# "EXCITING . . . INSPIRING"
### —*Real War Magazine*

Perhaps no words can ever recapture the
guts and glory of those heroic battles of
World War II when everything seemed
lost . . . and then the first Allied victories
came . . . and finally we rolled on
to V-E Day, and V-J Day.

But here is one book that has been called
"an honor roll of those finest hours."
It is written from on-the-spot descriptions
. . . some of them by the Germans and
Japanese who were our enemies then
. . . and it is compiled by the Combat
Historian of the U. S. General Staff.

Here is the diary of a war generation, and as you
read these pages . . . "You are there . . ."

# HEROIC
# BATTLES
## OF WORLD WAR II

Compiled by

## Major Howard Oleck

*Combat Historian, U.S. General Staff*

**WILDSIDE PRESS**

# CONTENTS

# DIARY OF A NAZI PILOT

## By Hans Prenger

[*The personal diary of a Luftwaffe pilot, Hans Prenger, was found at the Flak Kaserne near Hilden, Germany in 1945. Never before translated or published, the following diary extracts offer a revealing insight into the mind of a Nazi flyer. The diary was written partly in the German Stolze-Schrey shorthand system.*

*Hans Prenger was the Observer-Commander of a Heinkel bomber when the Germans attacked in the early days of World War II. His rank then was Oberleutnant (1st Lieutenant), and finally, was Group Leader of a Fernkampfgruppe (Long Range Group).*]

MAY 15, 1940: My crew are all top men. *Oberfeldwebel* (Flight Sergeant) Manfred Schmidt is my pilot. Corporal Rolf Wegener is my rear gunner. Radioman is Siegfried Koellmann, *Obergefreiter* (Private First Class). And gunner, *Feldwebel* Seuthe.

My ship is a Heinkel, after all. I had hoped for a JU (Junkers). So be it! If the Fuehrer ordered me to fly in a fruit box, I would obey.

*May 24, 1940:* We take off every morning with fighter escort. Our escorts are good, tough ME's (Messerschmitts). Regular bombing missions all around the western front—Rotterdam, Metz, Brussels, and a dozen other targets. Today we laid our eggs on the railroad yards at Nancy. Plenty of flak, but no hits on any of our planes. Rotten bad anti-aircraft shooting. The Frenchmen must have been very nervous.

Everytime I work the bomb release, I silently say a a little phrase to those below: "Greetings from the Fatherland. A German greeting to you." It amuses me great-

7

ly. I doubt that those below are amused. But surely *interested*. It makes me chuckle inside myself.

*May 26, 1940:* Today it was Amsterdam. Very low-level bombing. People running around with baby carriages in the streets. Many pedal bicycles. We strafe after dropping our bombs. It is very exhilarating. Like toys they look, or like silly ants, running around in circles, and flopping around when we strafe. They learn soon that they cannot escape from us. This will teach them what it means to attack the German people. A sharp lesson we teach.

*May 27, 1940:* Wegener troubles me. He questions the strafing of civilians. The man needs discipline. I explained to him that all the enemies of the Fuehrer are people born to be slaves, who must either bow the knee or taste German steel. He had better stop questioning our tactics. After all, I have a low National Socialist Party number, and thus a high duty to correct error in any German.

*May 28, 1940:* Bombed a French airfield today. Destroyed three Moranes on the ground. Not one Frenchy could get up in the air to argue with us. They are a decadent race, the Frenchies. To think that these are the people who once produced a Napoleon! Now they are good only to serve the Master Race.

Strafed thick crowds of people on the French roads. They wanted war, eh! We'll give them war! Not a bullet wasted with such thick-packed crowds of people. So many Frenchies less to eat food that could be used by Germans.

*May 29, 1940:* We saw a drop of our parachute troops near Amsterdam. Some Dutchmen fired at our parachute men while they were floating down. Typical, cowardly democratic conduct—shooting at helpless men in parachutes. It disgusts me. But we taught the Dutchmen a lesson by fire-bombing the suburban towns the same evening.

*May 30, 1940:* We struck *Duenkirchen* (Dunkerque) today. One great mass of flame and great columns of black smoke. A wonderful sight. My ship was rocked by the concussions of explosions below on the ground. The fury of the Teuton! Let the world see, and take care!

*June 2, 1940:* Crowds of English Tommies on the shallows at Duenkirchen today. We went after them, but a swarm of Hurricanes appeared suddenly. Big dogfights between our ME's and the Hurricanes. We caught one boat full of Tommies and our bombs turned it over. The water was full of Tommies trying to swim ashore. We strafed the swimmers again and again. We will make the English Channel truly English, full of dead Englishmen.

*June 4, 1940:* Bad luck. Disgustingly bad weather prevented us from striking Duenkirchen today. Where in hell do the damned English get all the boats and fighter planes there? They are very lucky—so far. But it won't help them. I am eager for good weather and a good killing time.

*June 5, 1940:* My good friend Oberleutnant Wilhelm Steutsel is dead. His Heinkel was shot down by a Hurricane over Duenkirchen. Gruss Gott, Wilhelm. A fine German warrior has gone to glorious death in battle. We shall strike down many a Briton in your memory, Wilhelm.

*July 8, 1940:* Ordered to Instrument School at Gatow.

*February 16, 1941:* Birmingham was the target today. We laid our eggs on a big factory there. Rotten bad weather. Soupy rain over the damned Channel. Very uncomfortable, with nothing to see but the faint green lights on the instrument panel. Ten ME's in box formation, below and on our flanks, escorted us. 5000 meters altitude, and very cold. I was busy with navigation calculations most of the time.

The damned Spitfires caught us on the way back. Flak had not been bad, going in. Coming out was another story. The English planes came out of the clouds like bees. I put the steel helmet on Veit's head and ordered the others to put on theirs. A mad series of dogfights were all around us. We lost five ME's and two Heinkels. Of course, we got fifteen or twenty of the Spitfires, according to the report of Group Leader Vorstmann.

Every mission now, when we return to our base, we find plenty of holes in our ship. So far, never a hit in a vital spot.

9

*April 23, 1941:* I notice that I feel very tired when we return from a mission. Terribly tired. A little only, while on the flights; but terribly tired coming back.

After interrogation and reports, when we return, it feels better. Plenty of good food and drink makes us feel better then. Having the night and next day off is soothing.

Our base, near Etampes, about 20 miles south of Paris, is very cosy. Plenty of champagne and cognac. Quite comfortable. But still I feel very tired.

*April 25, 1941:* Much talk again about the invasion of England soon. The Fuehrer will finish off the English soon now. I understand that many new shallow-draft boats are being built for the invasion.

*May 4, 1941:* Found a fine painting in a shop in Paris today. The dealer wanted a high price. He took what I offered, in scrip, when I suggested that the Gestapo might be interested in his collection. I sent the picture to my cousin, Lise.

*May 8, 1941:* Well, well! We got a group of HD girls assigned to the village for our boys, today. (HD means *Helferinnen vom Dienst;* uniformed women's auxiliary, clerical workers; their main function—to "aid and *comfort"* the German troops. Later, supplemented by official brothels in which girls of conquered nations were forced to serve the German troops).

Of course, I personally prefer a Frenchwoman. There's more zest to that, especially if she needs to be forced just a little bit. But for most German soldiers it is well to have the HD girls handy, like a touch of home.

A German soldier is entitled to enjoy the women of a conquered nation. That is a proper trophy of war. Inferior races, like the French, Poles, or Jews, can serve the Master Race's comfort and pleasure. That's what they *will do,* too—serve us.

*June 2, 1941:* My crew is becoming tired and too tense. Some quarreling among them. I hear them on the intercom. Nerves tight, I suppose. The pig-dog Spitfires! But I cannot help admiring the Tommies. Good flyers. They make it hot for us.

On the bombing run over London today one Spitfire was especially troublesome. I was peering through the bombsight, calling out "Ata" (right or "Imi" (left) (like the American "Roger" or "Baker," phonetic code used for clarity). Gemeiner yelled that this English plane kept following us. Then he became silent. He was hit in the face by a bullet. Alive when we got back, but his face is shattered. Very upsetting to the crew. Much blood.

Our new rear gunner is Corporal Piet Manschfeld. He is an ardent Party member. I hope that he is as good a gunner as he is a National Socialist.

*June 26, 1941:* Last night, I took one of the HD women. An officer-level girl, of course. Her name is Inge. Not very pretty, really, but anxious to please. It was very disappointing. She talked like a Party lecturer. If there is a child, the State will care for it. After all, I am pure Aryan and so is Inge. But it depressed me. Good eugenics is one thing, but this cold breeding is too much like a stud farm. Even so, of course, if Herr Goebbels and the Fuehrer approve this, naturally, I believe it to be wise and good.

If there is a child, I will not know whether it is mine or that of another officer. Thus I feel nothing for Inge at all. It is rather confusing.

*July 2, 1941:* Flak caught the port engine, over Manchester, today. It went down to 1600, and then down to 1200. The ship was pulling badly. We got back all right, but Manschfeld vomited all over the tail. Now the stink there is strong. The HE is all right, though. Just a pushed-in fuel line. Ground crew fixed it in a few minutes.

*July 16, 1941:* I understand that the English are in a panic. No wonder, the way we have been smashing them! The Luftwaffe is showing them who is master. I am proud to be one of Germany's airmen—one of the Third Reich's Knights of the Skies.

*July 23, 1941:* My request for new JU planes has been refused. But we are getting new HE's. So we will continue to fly our good old HE's. I am getting a short leave soon, and then am to attend a school. Perhaps a promotion again. *Hauptman* (Captain) is a good grade, but I have earned more, it seems. Perhaps there will be another promotion. The Fuehrer recognizes faithful service. I have flown over forty missions already.

11

*July 29, 1941:* In hospital as I write this. We crashed on returning from a mission after shipping in the Channel area. Veit was plainly nervous and tense on the return, and I half-expected a bad landing. My right leg is badly broken. No other men hurt, other than scratches and bruises.

Now my promotion may be delayed. But I cannot complain about the rest. The nurses are very attentive. There is one especially, named Anna, who interests me. We shall see.

I probably will limp for a time, the doctors say. Ground duty for me, when I am out of hospital. In a way, I am not sorry.

*January 2, 1942:* So the Americans are in the war too, now. We'll show those decadent swine what it means to annoy the Germans. As soon as we finish off the English, which is any day now, we'll teach the Yankee pigs a hard lesson.

This may yet be a most important event for me. When we have conquered America there will be *Gauleiter* (Governor) posts in plenty. I rather like the thought of being Gauleiter over one of the States. And why not? I have earned it.

*August 3, 1942:* The new crewmen are different from the old crew. Nobody laughs or sings, or tells stories. It is the same with all the crews. So many old friends are gone, never to return.

Things are different now. We all used to be *crews*—close friends. Now, all are just five men in one ship, hardly talking. There is some wondering about when this all will end. But we Germans fight on—forever, if the Fuehrer commands.

Yesterday, I was called to the *Gefechtstand* (Headquarters) of *Reichsmarschall* Goering himself. The chateau is not far from Etampes. The Field Marshall himself pinned the Iron Cross on my tunic. "Our Hermann" is a true German, hearty and vigorous, his cursing and great appetite the marks of a virile spirit.

There is no doubt that Goering understands that the RAF is a tough foe. The Americans, too, are strong fighters, as far as we have met them. The *Feldzeitung*

(*Field News*—like the American *Stars and Stripes*) tells only a little of what we know about the strength of our enemies.

*August 17, 1942:* The damned Americans bombed Rouen railroad yards today. This was the first time American bombers were seen. We understand that they flew in English planes, up to now. The pigs bomb their own Frenchy friends!

*September 1, 1942:* A new American fighter plane has appeared. It is called a P-38. Very fast and maneuverable. But when the Americans face German guns it will not help them.

*September 29, 1942:* Guests for dinner today. Three flyers from an American bomber that was shot down near Le Mans. Several French peasants who tried to hide the Yankees were executed, of course. The Americans were questioned here, but gave no useful information.

Strange people, the Americans. They didn't seem to be afraid of us. As though a piece of bad luck had interfered with their business. They were annoyed with themselves. Very unsoldierly in their manner. You'd think they were truly guests, from the way they lounge about.

Naturally, we'll break the Americans and the English. But you must give them credit. They will not be easy to conquer.

We told them that we hold captured airmen to be, like ourselves, something better than plain ground soldiers. One of the Yankees said that he became a flyer because "he didn't like marching," and laughed. I do not understand such queer ideas. These people are not like us. They do not seem to put their hearts into war, nor enjoy it. They get no joy out of destroying a foe. They seem to do it as though it were an unpleasant task.

Perhaps that is why we beat them so easily. I can see why we Germans are superior to them, and destined to rule them.

One of the Americans saw an HD girl who came into the mess room. He stared at her legs and winked at her. No breeding nor manners. Pigs—that is what the Americans are. We shall teach them better manners.

*October 3, 1942:* I hear that Inge had a child last

13

spring. Haven't seen nor heard from her. It leaves me very cold. I have no interest in it. There are more important things to think about and to do. But at least I have done my duty to continue the Master Race.

*January 28, 1943:* American planes have bombed Wilhelmshaven. Over seventy B-17's bombed the city yesterday. What barbarism, to bomb a defenseless city of no military importance! They truly are uncultured swine, trying to smash a civilization far superior to anything they can understand.

*February 11, 1943:* We entertained a group of flyers from the *Pik A* group today. (*Pik A* means "Ace of Spades"—the *Richthofen Squadron,* top fighter squadron of the Luftwaffe). The great Majors von Maltzahn, Wick and Moelders were not here. The *Pik A's* have destroyed over 1000 enemy planes in Poland, France, Belgium, Holland, and England.

What a wonderful team we are, such fighter groups as the *Pik A,* our bombers, and all the other superb German warriors of the sky!

*February 26, 1943:* Nielander is a Gestapo agent in our group, as I have known for some time. There may be traitors anywhere, even in the Luftwaffe. He, and other Himmler men, are watchful to weed out any men infected with the bacillus of democracy. He is suspicious of some of the crewmen, who he says are not as enthusiastic as they should be, in the Fatherland's defense.

*March 25, 1943:* My brother Paul is dead, killed by American bombers at Vegesack Submarine Base last week. God damn the Yankees to hell for killing such a fine German sea warrior. Paul's death notice mentioned his Gold Medal of Honor and Silver National Socialist Party Cross for Merit. It said that fate "did not permit him the joy of seeing final victory."

I am deeply depressed. When shall I see "the joy of final victory?"

*April 7, 1943:* I was ordered to flying duty again, today. My bad leg still causes me to limp. But as Group Leader I do not fly the plane and my leg is of no importance. But if we are shot down, I am slow-moving and clumsy. Will I be able to bail out quickly, if need arises?

14

*April 10, 1943:* Mission over the channel today, against shipping. The air was full of Spitfires and P-38's. Never have I seen so many, and such persistence. The Americans are very aggressive and hard to shake off. We lost too many escorting ME's—far too many. We were harried and attacked without pause. It is not like the old days. When we returned, my hands were trembling. I am very tired. It is hard to write. What is the matter with me! When I saw all the bullet holes in the ship, back at the base, I became wet with cold sweat. Can it be that my nerve is cracking?

*April 12, 1943:* So many old friends are gone! Today I saw Putzi Hesse go down in flames over the channel. We were at Gatow flying school together. So many are gone! So few of us old-timers are left! How much longer can I last? I wonder. Sixty-three missions already. How many can a man take?

The English were tough enough, but the American fighters are worse. They seem to be so coldly determined to destroy us. So damned persistent! I returned from a routine mission to Southampton, quivering and shaking. The crew were grey of face. We lost three HEs' out of our seven. It is terrifying to think of the future.

God help me. I am afraid!

*April 14, 1943:* Today I was reprimanded by high headquarters. Quite unjustly, I believe. My "group" of eight bombers was flying towards London. Over the channel, we were met by swarms of Spitfires and P-38's. *Swarms. Over sixty* that I could count myself. They attacked and shot down *all, every one* of our ten ME escorts. *All ten.* Then they attacked my bombers.

I ordered the group to turn back for home. What choice did I have? Even so, the Americans and Tommies shot down two of my HE's. We were lucky to have *any* of us get back. I could hardly walk when we returned.

Is this cowardice?

Should a man be reprimanded for *this*?

*April 16, 1943:* Mission today, a sweep over the channel. We saw nothing. Did nothing. Returned by noon.

I am not well. I cannot sleep much now. Nerves are too tight. Smoke and drink too much.

When will it all end?

*[Note: It all ended for Hans Prenger on his next mission. Research in Luftwaffe records revealed that his Heinkel bomber exploded in midair in a dogfight over the English Channel on April 18, 1943.]*

# I WATCHED HAMBURG DIE

## By Ernest Hecht

FOURTEEN YEARS AGO, I saw a whole city turn into a funeral pyre. It was the most horrifying sight I have ever witnessed—so terrible that it was almost impossible for the human mind to accept.

The city was Hamburg, one of the largest industrial centers of Hitler's Third Reich—and I was one of the instruments of its death.

For I was an American spy, assigned by the OSS to set up the city of Hamburg for complete destruction. I was raised and schooled in Germany, and spoke the language without an accent, so I was the perfect man for the job. Also, I had the added advantage for my role of having only one arm, so I was able to pose as a disabled veteran of the Afrika Corps, a former member of the 15th Panzer Grenadier Regiment. I was supplied with a card that showed me to be qualified to drive military vehicles. Thus, I was able to obtain a job driving a truck in the city.

I worked alone, above suspicion, and free to move about among the city's defenses. Once a month, I reported by radio to London. It was a perfect arrangement, but one slip would mean death before a firing squad as an Allied spy.

On the night of July 25, 1943, I shut down my illegal short-wave radio for the last time and prepared to return to my own section of the city before the police arrived —they surely had the radio zeroed in by then. On the way, I stopped as usual at Meisner's café for a schnapps. There, I met my friend, Peter Dressen, and we played several games of checkers. While we played, I wondered when the raids would begin. I also wondered what Dres-

17

sen would say if I should suddenly tell him that I was an American.

A little after midnight, when I left the café and started for home, the night was still warm. The city was blacked out as usual, and I walked slowly along the narrow streets. A few blocks from the flat where I lived, I was stopped by the wail of the sirens.

I hurried to the nearest shelter. It was already crowded when I arrived. The harassed citizens hoped to insure themselves of a night's sleep. I found a spot on a wooden bench and sat down, looking about me at the clutter of men, women and children.

Then my heart started to pound for I knew that the complete destruction of Hamburg, the hub of Germany's industrial machine, was about to begin. I heard a dull thud and checked my watch. It was exactly thirty-three minutes past midnight.

Next to me was a dried-up old man who looked like the kaiser. I wondered if he would die. Ahead of me was a young girl with a baby. I wondered about her, too. That is one of the difficulties of being a spy. A soldier in the line kills or is killed. He trains his guns on an impersonal enemy. The men in the Navy seldom ever see their target and the Air Force takes an even less personal part in their destruction. But the spy is right on the spot. His job makes it imperative that he befriend the very people he is plotting to destroy. It is hard on the individual.

I sat there thinking: "I have been with you people for a year. Some of you are my friends. And in the next few days you will be destroyed. I helped in the destruction. What do you think of me now?"

I closed my eyes and tried to think of London, gutted and burned by German bombers; Swansea, Wales, a small city of gentle, friendly people—completely destroyed by German bombs. Portsmouth and Manchester—I thought of all the places that the Germans had battered relentlessly without a thought for human suffering. I thought of the labor camps, the gas chambers, the oppressive tentacles of the Nazi war machine. To destroy Hamburg would

18

speed the end of the war and put an end to Nazi infamies.

But when I opened my eyes I still couldn't fully rationalize the deaths of these people around me. I left the shelter and stood in the street, watching the raid.

The bombers, big British Lancasters, came in two waves of 300 each. The raid had been planned for over a year, and the pilots came in with uncanny precision. They first dropped the thousands upon thousands of tin foil strips that fouled the Nazi radar screens and virtually crippled the radar-controlled ack-ack. They centered the attack on the hub of the city, dropping high explosives and incendiaries. The fury of the attack rocked the Germans, but it was only the beginning.

When the raid was over, there were 1500 dead, and much of the city was in flames. The Reich declared a state of emergency, and supplies were ordered rushed in from other cities.

The next afternoon, before the fires were under control, the sirens screamed again. Through the dense clouds of smoke that still swirled over Hamburg, a squadron of 180 flying fortresses of the 8th Air Force made a high-altitude raid on the port area, hitting with deadly precision.

My hard-gained reports were having their effect. The Allies seemed to know more about Hamburg than the Reich.

This was one of the best-defended cities in the world. The metropolis was under a shroud of darkness every night. Heavy anti-aircraft batteries and thousands of fighter planes were always on the alert. A total of 137 air raids had done little damage to the city's industry which kept producing under a heavy veil of camouflage.

Three thousand factories, producing everything from munitions to boots, were on round-the-clock production. Hundreds of ships jammed the wharves, loading supplies for the troops in western and northern Europe. The U-boat construction yards were turning out a sub a day.

But the city was not invulnerable, as the Germans in their insane arrogance believed. Despite the firewalls and incendiary-proof ceilings of the factories, the best water

19

supply in all Germany, the efficient and methodical fire department that boasted 3400 men, 288 modern trucks and 36 fireboats, it took the Royal Air Force only ten days to reduce Hamburg to a smouldering wasteland that reeked with the rotting corpses of 80,000 people.

The Achilles heel of the industrial center was its age. Typical of European cities, the center of Hamburg was actually a medieval town of narrow streets and houses built close together, five stories high. Around this section was an eighteenth-century town of much the same pattern, but with higher buildings framed and floored with wood. And scattered throughout these areas were the usual small industries, with yards loaded with flammable trash. I had reported that fire in this area could have a devastating effect.

I had no idea that the effect would reach the hellish proportions that followed.

The second morning after the first midnight raid, the sirens wailed again and the 8th Air Force was back with another softening dose of high-explosive blockbusters. They came in with fifty-seven planes and completely disabled the Neuhof power plant, a vital link in the city's life line.

For the rest of the day the British sent in small groups of fast attack bombers that only roared over the city, dropping no bombs, but setting off the sirens and unnerving the citizens.

At midnight of the 26th, the RAF attack started in earnest. The city had been shaken and the people's nerves were taxed to the breaking point. Eight hundred four-engined Lancasters zoomed out of the skies in waves from every direction, centering their assault on the "old town." The first wave dropped incendiaries, then when the fire-fighting crews rushed from their shelters to squelch the flames, the next wave roared in and dropped high explosives, sending the fire-fighters racing for cover. The pattern was repeated until thousands of small fires had grown into one surging avalanche of flame.

It was estimated that in the three major raids that leveled the city, the British and American planes dropped 1200 huge land mines, 3,000,000 stick incendiaries,

20

25,000 high-explosive bombs, 80,000 phosphorus and small incendiary bombs, 5,000 large liquid incendiaries, 500 flares and 500 phosphorus cannisters.

The city went up in flames, spreading unchecked, and setting almost every building within a five-mile radius ablaze.

The tremendous heat from the fire center created an updraft that produced a partial vacuum, sucking in fresh oxygen from the surrounding areas to feed the spreading flames and increasing the updraft to gale force until a bellows-like phenomenon was whipping oxygen into the fire with hurricane velocity.

The nightmare that this created is nearly impossible to envision. Within an hour, the perimeter of the fire was being whipped by 100-mile-an-hour-winds, a typhoon that swept everything before it into the center of the fire that was now raging at 2,000 degrees above zero. Human beings, animals, anything that was not tied down, were snatched up and hurled into the inferno.

The narrow, winding streets and alleys became channels of death, soaring with huge wind-lashed sheets of flame, the buildings collapsing as the flames grew ever higher until a tidal wave of fire belched upwards out of the core of the blaze that reached a height of three miles, a gigantic fire spout a mile in diameter.

As the heat of the blaze increased, the air shelters became ovens. Unable to stand the suffocating heat, the inhabitants of many shelters flung open the doors and poured into the flaming streets. The moment they stepped into the gale, they were sent sprawling, tumbling and screaming into the relentless inferno. Even those who managed to grasp something and resist the powerful wind soon burst into flames where they clung, from the intense heat.

Thousands of people, their clothing in flames, leaped shrieking into the canals that run through the city. They were forced to stay submerged for hours, constantly ducking their burned faces beneath the water to stay alive.

Those who remained in the shelters fared little better. Packed in like sardines, most of them soon succumbed to the heat, and days later their roasted bodies were found rotting in heaps.

When that horrible inferno first erupted, I found myself near a small park. I ran to a fountain that commemorated the Hitler Youth Movement and plunged into the water. As I clung to the metal railing, I saw a woman run from a shelter with two children. The hurricane winds wrenched the two small children from her grasp, and as she clutched the rungs of an iron fence, staring with numbed horror, her children were lifted into the air and flung into the depths of the fire.

I saw an elderly man and his wife struggling along the street, battling the wind. As he grasped a small tree for support, his wife was torn from his hand. Screaming with horror, he watched, helplessly, as she was dragged off into the flames.

I turned away, sickened, and looked up at the statue above the fountain. A young boy and girl, their marble chins defiant and cruel, stood together, their arms outstretched in the Nazi salute. And then I looked about me at the holocaust. This was what Hitler had brought to the Germans. A megalomaniac who wanted to rule the world, he had taught them to destroy all those who would stand for freedom. And now they must be destroyed to end the Nazi nightmare.

Adding to the flaming terror were the phosphorus bombs. As they struck and exploded, they sent out a shower of burning phosphorus that stuck to everything —human flesh as well as wood and metal. People ran shrieking through the streets, literally burning alive, as the fiery, phosphorus crusts ate into their bodies.

Those who were able to reach the canals, plunged in to extinguish the terrible flames. But their relief was momentary. Although phosphorus will not burn under water, the moment it is exposed to air, it bursts into flame again. A hand raised from the water instantly became a torch.

The phosphorus victims in the canals had to stay immersed, with only their mouths above water. But the intense heat spread over the surface of the canals, the flying sparks and hot ash forced many of them to climb

22

out to escape the awful ordeal of the water, and they burned to death on the banks.

Others succumbed to the heat, and their tortured heads sank below the surface of the water and disappeared.

For several days, these victims of the phosphorus bombs stayed in the water. As the fires were slowly reduced and the gales subsided, friends and relatives flocked to the canals to offer help. The air was filled with the agonizing screams and moans of scorched and dying people, and the anguished cries of relatives who could offer no solace. The pain of the phosphorus burns increased daily, as the wounds festered and skin peeled away.

Finally, the police evacuated the area, and that night, a troop of soldiers moved in with clubs and rifles. The crack of automatics was heard late into the night as the machine-like Nazi efficiency again took its toll of human life. By morning, the canals were cleared.

When it seemed that nothing further could happen to the people of Hamburg, the British attacked again. Just before midnight, on July 29th, while the center of the city still was burning, the bomb-laden Lancasters roared in. To the horror and despair of the stunned populace, it was the heaviest raid thus far.

This time the RAF went after the suburban areas— Rotherbaum, St. Georg, Bambeck, Havestude, Ulenhorst, Ependorf, Winterhude.

More than a thousand bombers delivered death to these previously undamaged areas, and the scene of July 26th was repeated with far greater intensity. The terrible hurricane gales swept entire cities. Barmbeck, a densely-populated area, was reduced to ashes.

This time, I was in the center of Ulenhorst, and although I escaped with minor burns, the loss of most of my hair and eyebrows, I witnessed the flaming horror that enveloped a whole city.

On August 2nd, the British returned with 300 heavy bombers to deliver the final death blow. The sirens wailed their terrifying dirge above the roar of the still-burning city as the huge planes droned through the smoke-darkened skies. This time, however, the city was spared the centralized attack. The air above the city was so hot, the winds so strong, that the bombers had to scatter and spread their loads over a wide area from high altitude.

This was the last attack.

In the chaos that followed, I took the opportunity to escape from the city. I made my way to Switzerland and subsequently reported for a new assignment, but behind me, Hamburg was still in flames, an area of total destruction.

By August 4th, the fires had consumed everything combustible within the city and finally began to subside. But it was two days before rescue workers could enter the smoldering ruins.

The complete picture, the grand finale, is depicted in a report to the German High Command which fell into American hands following the fall of the Third Reich:

"The streets were covered with thousands of corpses— mothers with their children, youths, old men. Naked, with a waxen pallor like dummies in a shop window, they lay in every posture, quiet and peaceful or cramped, the death struggle shown in the expression on their faces. The shelters showed the same picture, even more horrible in effect, as it showed in many cases the final distracted struggle against a merciless fate. In other shelters the position of remains of bones and skulls showed how the occupants had fought to escape from their buried prison.

"Thick glass bottles melted, streams of molten kitchen utensils, cast-iron and pieces of tile as well as a superficial layer of ashes of soft burnt brick, give some idea of the high temperature which had been obtained.

"The stench of advanced decomposition pervaded whole districts."

The destruction was complete; Hamburg never rose again during the war.

Germany's Minister of Propaganda, Joseph Goebbels, wrote in his diary: ". . . a catastrophe the extent of which simply staggers the imagination."

And as the flames died out in Hamburg, so did the

flame of Fascism die out across Germany. The British had the formula for German defeat and they poured it on. Dresden was next, completely destroyed in a single mammoth raid, 110,000 persons killed, and Berlin was next.

I will never forget the horror that was Hamburg, but I shudder to think of the years of horror that might have been if German industry had not been completely crippled by those terrible raids. It is difficult for an American to envision the inhuman crimes, the ghastly tortures, the bestial murders that the Nazi war machine visited upon their conquered victims. Destroying this machine actually was an act of mercy—it saved countless millions from terror and death.

# BISMARCK SEA

### By Tetsuko Mikotoya
### Ensign, Imperial Japanese Navy

THE VERY SEA ITSELF seemed to be spouting flame and roaring death! Tons of explosives rained down on our stricken vessels, sending great geysers of water filled with fragments of steel high into the air.

The blasts slammed and thundered against the hulls of our disabled ships. Plates buckled and ripped open. Men who clambered out on the open decks, seeking safety from flooding holds or bursting steam lines were torn to pieces by hails of machine gun bullets hosed from the wing guns of the strafing planes.

Even those who managed to launch lifeboats or rafts were butchered as they bobbed amid the tangles of wreckage covering the blood-reddened sea.

It was sheer slaughter—a massacre at sea practically unparalleled in all the history of no-quarter warfare.

We didn't have a chance! Most of our anti-aircraft guns had been wrecked; smashed or torn from their mounts by the force of the bomb-blasts. It would have made little difference even if the guns had still been in working order—we had been without ammunition for several hours.

There was absolutely nothing we could do to protect ourselves from the continuous, savage onslaughts of the American and Australian aircraft. The handful of vessels that remained out of the huge convoy could not even take evasive action. All had been damaged and refused to respond properly to their helms.

Standing on the shattered bridge of the *Asagumo*, I heard the engine room report the failure of all but one engine. The message that came over the speaker tube could hardly be heard above the roar of the diving planes and the ear-splitting chatter of their guns.

After a quick consultation with the commander of the destroyer, Lieutenant Omori, I gave the engineers their orders. "Maintain as much engine speed as possible!"

The forward deck was a shambles, littered with the mangled bodies of more than a score of our crew. Some of them had been blown to pieces when the 500-pound bomb struck on the port side. Others had been cut down by strafing fighters.

A few more moments of howling, shrieking hell passed. Then the attacking planes, their bombs and bullets gone, banked into the sun and flew back to their bases to refuel and rearm.

"We have half an hour," Lt. Omori said to no one in particular. "The next time they come back we will join the others . . ."

His voice trailed off and I saw that he was ashen-faced and trembling. But the reaction was not caused by fear, for Lt. Omori was a brave officer. He was overcome by the awful horror of our predicament, by the terrible carnage we had seen—and would doubtless see again when the enemy aircraft returned.

We both knew of the hideous track that we had been leaving astern us in the Bismarck Sea. Our faltering propellors churned an unsteady wake that led back—*through miles of water thick and slimy with oil and blood.*

Corpses of nearly 5,000 Japanese soldiers and sailors were floating on the waves behind us. They had been killed in the savage slaughter that had claimed thirteen vessels out of our seventeen-ship convoy in less than twenty-four hours!

All the transports were gone—blown to shreds by bombs or sent to the bottom by aerial torpedoes. There had been nine of them, loaded with supplies and troops . . .

*Teiyo-Maru — Shinano-Maru — Kokoku-Maru — Aiyo — Oigawa-Maru — Kenbu-Maru — Taimei-Maru — No-jima — Kyokusei-Maru . . .*

They had all been sunk, spewing the dead and dying from their ruptured hulls as they went down—flinging chunks of human flesh into the air as they exploded.

But our losses had not ended there. Eight destroyers of our flotilla had been assigned to guard the convoy. The ships were all modern, manned by veterans of the Pacific naval battles. Eight destroyers had been considered an *ample force* to protect nine transports.

The Allied warplanes had sunk the others. The bodies of our comrades aboard the *Tokitsukaze, Arashio, Asashio* and *Shirayuki* added to the grisly flotsam of the annihilated transports.

Ironically, we had come very close to completing our dangerous voyage without a single incident. On the afternoon of March 2nd, we were less than two days' sailing time from our destination—Salamaua, New Guinea. We steamed ahead steadily, secure in the knowledge that we ran little risk of observation from the air.

Our convoy, destroyers forming a box screen around the transports, plowed through the heavy swells beneath a heavy, menacing weather front. Rain poured down in sheets—there was reason to believe that a nasty squall was not far off.

All day, "Negative submarine contact," had been the report from the seamen manning our undersea listening devices.

"Little fear of the Americans leaving their bases today," I observed, scanning the black sky with a smile. "We'll reach New Guinea without difficulty." My relief grunted something in agreement. He was still a bit sleepy, having just been awakened for his watch. I drew on my oilskin coat and went below.

The *Asagumo*, like destroyers the world over, rolled and pitched violently in any but the calmest of calm seas. I had to hold tightly, bracing myself against the railing on deck and on the ladder as I went below.

No sooner had I entered the tiny wardroom which I shared with two other junior officers, when a seaman summoned me to return to the bridge. When I stepped out on deck again, I was surprised. As sometimes happens

28

with the unpredictable weather in the Pacific, a weird phenomenon had occurred.

Suddenly, a huge gap had opened in the thick cloud layers. The late afternoon sun shone through the vast opening. On both sides of us, the skies still remained dark and threatening, but directly overhead there was only clear, azure blue. I paused to stare at the sight for only a moment, and then proceeded to the bridge.

"Bombers! American planes!" Lt. Omori shouted excitedly when I reached the ship's control room. He pointed off our starboard bow and I could see three distant, dark blobs. Powerful binoculars brought them close enough for identification as American air force B-24's!

Already, the order for "battle stations" had been given. Sailors were racing along the decks to their gun positions. The barrels of our anti-aircraft weapons were already swivelling toward the heavens, ready to track any attacking enemy craft. We were ready for the bombers—*but no attack came.*

As suddenly as they had opened up, the clouds above us closed—almost as though they were double doors that someone had slammed shut. The B-24's disappeared from view.

"They didn't have much time to observe," I said hesitantly. "I doubt if they could have seen us . . ."

"It doesn't make much difference," Lt. Omori shrugged. "We're under the weather front again. The reports we've been getting indicate the heavy clouding exists in a solid front all the way to Salamaua."

We secured from battle stations and I returned below. Nothing happened in the hours that followed, and I dismissed the incident from my mind.

Dawn broke—grim and grey, with only a few distant shards of sunlight cracking the overcast in isolated patches. But even this was enough to give us concern. It indicated that the weather front was not as solid and far-reaching as we had believed . . .

The weather situation grew progressively worse—from our standpoint—in the first hour after dawn. The cloud front was breaking up with comparative speed. There

29

were several great clear patches of sky showing now. But we were still fairly optimistic. We knew that the Americans and Australians had been building up their land-based air strength in the New Guinea area, but we believed that our own planes, located on a string of nearby fields, could easily cope with the threat.

This steadily increasing enemy air power was the main reason we were making our convoy run. Our 51st Division, fighting in the Lee-Salamaua sector, had been badly mauled by Australian troops and American soldiers of the 32nd Infantry Division. Because of the surprisingly large number of airplanes which they flew in constant support of their ground forces, the Allies had practically decimated the 51st Division.

The transports in our convoy were loaded with more than 5,000 troop-reinforcements for the 51st, along with much needed fuel, ammunition and supplies.

It was not unlikely that the Allies would attempt aerial attacks on the convoy—*if they spotted us.* On the other hand, we could rely on our anti-aircraft armament and Zero fighters based at Rabaul, Buin and other strategic points. The Zeros could come to our aid quickly if we were attacked.

At least this was our train of thought an hour after daybreak on the morning of March 3, 1943. But our illusions were shattered in the maelstrom that followed almost immediately!

*"Enemy aircraft approaching! Battle stations!"*

The warning rang through all the ships of convoy and escort. It was different than it had been the previous afternoon—there was a portentous urgency to the words. . . .

The patrolling B-24's *had* seen us! They had radioed our location to Allied air headquarters. The RAF and the American 5th Air Force had plenty of time during the night—plenty of time to plan the massive blow which fell on us!

Already, the heavy-caliber dual-purpose guns aboard the *Arashio* and *Yukikaze,* the leading destroyers of our

30

screen, were firing! They were blasting at the swarms of enemy planes that roared down on our ships.

"*Open fire!*"

The command was given aboard the *Asagumo* and our own anti-aircraft artillery opened up. I felt the destroyer shudder under my feet as the rapidly firing weapons vainly attempted to throw up a curtain of steel to protect the transports.

"Break radio silence! Call for the Zeros!" Lt. Oromi ordered. He took a great responsibility upon himself. He was not the convoy commander, nor even the senior naval officer in the escort. Nonetheless, he risked severe punishment when he saw that the command-vessel was under heavy attack. It had apparently been disabled in the first seconds of the assault.

"Captain Otami's communications may be inoperative," he explained hurriedly. "We must take the chance of asking for assistance. . . ." His voice was shaking.

We could not question the wisdom of his decision—the air was filled with hostile aircraft. They came from all sides. Our gunners were confronted with dozens—scores —of hurtling, diving, twisting targets!

There were planes of all types. Giant B-17's and B-24's lumbered high above, releasing tons upon tons of explosives! B-25 medium bombers bored in, dumping their 500-pound missiles. Fast attack planes and dive-bombers thundered down to bridge-level and strafed the decks of transports and destroyers after salvoing their bombs.

"We are under attack!" I scrawled into the log of the *Asagumo*. "Estimated strength of enemy force is between ninety and one hundred aircraft of all types. . . ."

We were not prepared for the awful fury of the onslaught—there had been no warning. Certainly no one dreamed that the Allies would send such a huge force of planes against the convoy.

*(Note—At the time of this action, radar was one of the most closely guarded war secrets of the Allies. Originally developed by the British, it was made completely available to the United States. It was unknown by the Axis forces. It enabled Allied operational units to un-*

*cover enemy forces, even though they were totally con-
cealed by clouds and cover. But it permitted the Americans to take advantage of the same cover since the
enemy was not so well equipped. The convoy discussed
here was located by scout planes. From the moment it
was found, it was tracked continuously. All the time the
Japs felt safe, they were being set up for the death blow.
What the lack of radar meant is shown by the fact that the
Japanese, though they knew the route of the convoy,
were unable to locate it, or come to its aid. There's a lot
of space in the Pacific. It's easy to get lost there. The
Japs learned that lesson—the hard way!)*

*Shinano-Maru* was the first to go. The 4,000-ton transport, loaded with soldiers and drums of aviation fuel, was
hit by three 500-pound bombs almost simultaneously.
The ship exploded in a great ball of flame! The hull rose
from the water and appeared to break in half before
settling back—sinking instantly.

The captains of the other vessels attempted to take
evasive action, *but it was useless.* No matter which way
they turned or twisted, they found entire flights and
squadrons of enemy planes waiting to pounce on them!

At least three squadrons of twin-engined Lockheed
P-38 fighters bored in, out of the fast-rising sun. They
lanced down at the ships with their throttles wide open—
their guns spewing fire and death. The powerful fighters
sprayed the convoy with streams of .50-caliber bullets,
mercilessly gunning down sailors on the decks of the
transports and destroyers.

The unequal battle lasted all morning, and another
transport and a destroyer went down. The Allied planes returned to their bases and then came back, flying in re-
lays. *There were always attacking aircraft overhead.* . . .

Shortly before 1100 hours, a small flight of Zeros came
to our aid, but they could do little against the superior
numbers of enemy aircraft. Three were shot out of the
sky immediately. The remainder were forced to return
to their base.

*Asagumo* slackened its speed to pull some of the

burned and dazed survivors of *Kenbu-Maru* out of the water after the ship was blown apart. Even this rescue operation was conducted at great peril. The American A-20 and P-38 pilots roared in, their fuselages barely skimming the waves, their guns spewing death!

"We're dropping far behind," I warned Lt. Omori. "We'll only provide a target for the next flight of bombers. . . ."

Reluctantly, he gave the order to make full speed. We were forced to abandon many men in the sea in order to maintain some semblance of order in what remained of the convoy.

Then, almost miraculously, the weather closed shortly after noon. A heavy sea began to run and we were lashed by wind and rain. The planes were forced to return to their bases and we had a temporary respite—a lull during which we could assess our staggering losses.

A total of five transport ships had been sunk. Two destroyers had gone under beneath the hail of bombs—a third was burning and would sink at any moment. Every other vessel had sustained some damage. The decks of the remaining destroyers were crowded with wounded or the oil-coated survivors the crews had managed to pull, half-dead, from the ocean.

Throughout the entire afternoon and night, we heard aircraft engines far above us.

"They're tracking us," Lt. Omori said quietly, almost with resignation. His voice was flat and toneless, reflecting the exhaustion he shared with all of us. "They're using radar. Let's hope that the weather stays bad—or they'll be on us again in the morning."

Ominously, dawn broke through scattered clouds. *We didn't have long to wait.* In the first light, the enemy planes screamed down on us again.

We were less than one hundred miles from Salamaua, our goal, *but we might as well have been halfway around the globe.* There was no escape from the inferno! Hour after hour, the Allied planes pounded us. After firing their last rounds, our anti-aircraft guns fell silent.

By nightfall, there were only two transports and five destroyers remaining. Our speed was cut to less than four knots. Desperately, we tried to save what was left—*but it was hopeless.* Then, torpedo boats came out from their lairs and added to the carnage!

The men who clung to life rafts or bobbed in the swells, clutching bits of wreckage, were strafed by fighter planes. Even the floating heaps of rubbish that covered the water were fair targets for the enemy pilots! They flew back and forth, *hosing bullets into everything.*

A 500-pound bomb struck our bow and killed almost every man in the gun crews. Even in death, they were draped across their useless weapons, fortunately the bomb was fused for instant detonation. Although it wreaked havoc above, it failed to penetrate below the waterline.

Almost half our crew was either dead or wounded. More than two hundred injured survivors of the other ships clustered above and below decks. Some were shrieking in horror—others groaned quietly—*or closed their eyes and waited for death.*

By morning of March 5, the destruction was complete. Not a single transport remained afloat. We still had four destroyers, but all were severely damaged and without ammunition.

Lt. Omori had to consult with the commanders of the other destroyers by semaphore—almost all radios had been wrecked by the bombings and strafings. The officers decided to try and make a run for Salamaua.

Evidently, the Allies were tired of their grisly sport, for we managed to reach port without further attack. The cost of our ordeal was unbelievable . . .

Nine transports and four destroyers had been sunk. We later learned that at least ten Zeros had been shot down by the enemy pilots—many more had been badly damaged. We were to learn weeks later that more than 150 Allied aircraft had been used in the attacks!

But the real loss was in the number of human lives that had been snuffed out. The waters of the Bismarck Sea carried a ghastly burden. Almost 5,000 men had been sacrificed. Their remains floated in the water, or were carried to the bottom in the blasted hulls of their ships.

It was vicious slaughter—*butchery.* Many of the victims

had been machine-gunned as they floundered helplessly in the sea. Many others drowned because the Allied airmen refused to halt their attack even while our destroyers were attempting to rescue survivors and injured men.

"Hundreds of our soldiers and sailors were *murdered,*" Lt. Omori wrote in his final report of the action.

I let his words speak for themselves. . . .

# THEY SERVED THEIR
# TIME IN HELL

### By Major Howard Oleck

IN A CORNER of the Marine cemetery on the western end of Guadalcanal there stands a faded wooden tombstone. It is a marker not for one particular grave, but for all. On the wooden board, words burned into the plank with a hot soldering iron are now barely legible. They say:

*"St. Peter—Let These Marines Enter Heaven—They Have Served Their Time In Hell—Guadalcanal."*

The man who burned those letters into the pathetic wooden tombstone spoke for all who had lived, suffered, and died on the dread island of Guadalcanal. That name is not a word, to the Marines and GIs who fought there. It is an emotion. In it are compressed the ultimate depths of horror, fear, sickness, hate, violence, disgust, and death. That is the real meaning of *Guadalcanal*. That weatherbeaten tombstone says it all.

Jungle war was new to the Americans who landed on "the 'Canal" in little Higgins boats. Coming ashore against no resistance, on the clustered islands of Tulagi, Gavutu and Guadalcanal, it began quietly enough. This was August 7, 1942, and some of the green Americans still wore old World War I helmets as they began the Solomon Islands invasion. Battalions from the 1st and 2nd Marine Divisions led the attack.

Incredible as it seems today, only a single Battalion of 2d Division Marines made the Tulagi assault landings. Another Battalion of the 1st Marines formed the original landing force for Guadalcanal. In all, less than 1000 men launched the first American invasion of enemy-held territory. Close behind them came thousands more.

Pure luck saved them from massacre. There were less than 1000 Japs on the island then. Pouring quickly ashore at Lunga Point, on the north shore of Guadalcanal, the Marines quickly seized an unfinished airfield there. Beyond it, they met and engaged the enemy troops, in the jungle and barren uplands, in what was to become a seemingly endless struggle.

Reinforcements began to pour in, for both sides. From Bougainville and Rabaul the Japs started the famous *Tokyo Express*. Every night destroyers and troopships landed more and more men, building the defense force faster than it could be destroyed. From Efate and New Hebrides the Americans brought in more shiploads of men of the 1st, 2nd and 10th Marines, and the Army's 25th Infantry Division and Americal Division.

The very day of the first landings, Japanese air and sea attacks began, in ever increasing violence. Determined to cut off the invaders' air and sea support, they threw whole fleets into the channel between Guadalcanal and Florida Islands. There, Yank and Jap forces grappled in deadly combat, almost daily. Over 50 warships, and hundreds of planes, sank in the death-filled narrows, to earn a grim new name for the 15-mile-wide sea lane— *Iron Bottom Channel*.

Ashore, the unfinished airfield, a muddy morass, formed the crude, sticky base (Henderson Field) for Marine air support. From it, obsolete P-40's, manned by ferociously brave pilots, soon were to take the air against overwhelmingly superior Jap planes—and shoot them out of the sky by sheer skill and courage.

First man to die was Private Russell L. Miller (New York City), of B Company, 2nd Marine Regiment. He was killed by a Jap bullet, at his Lewis Gun, on Florida Island. Right after that an American Navy shell, falling short, dropped on Miller's little assault group and wiped it out. The misery of the invasion had begun, on a typically rotten note.

On 'Canal, the Japanese quickly recovered from their surprise, and came forward to meet the invaders. Never before defeated, and full of propaganda about their invincibility, they hurled themselves on the Americans. Hys-

37

terical with almost religious ecstasy, they could not be stopped except by death. Here, for the first time, Americans faced combat with absolutely no choice but to kill or be killed.

In the jungle, death was everywhere. In hidden foxholes, behind trees, concealed in swamp hollows, or up in the trees, Japs waited. They were resigned to die if only they could shoot or grenade one American. Soon the Yanks learned the answer to those tactics as man after man fell, cut down by invisible snipers. Creeping and crawling forward, the Marines fired at every suspicious spot. They quickly learned to shoot first, and fast.

"Better waste a bullet on a coconut," said Sergeant Jim Tatum (Miami, Florida), "than save it and find the coconut was a Jap."

From the first minutes, the stinking rot of the jungle disgusted the men from the plains and mountains of America. Insects buzzed and crawled in swarms everywhere. Every man soon was covered with red, itching insect bites. And every man stayed that way. Sweat and filth became normal, and cleanliness was something only remembered from another world.

Swarming Jap ships in *Iron Bottom Channel* bombarded the Americans from the rear, while newly landed artillery and mortars smashed at them from the jungle. High above, atop Mt. Austen, overlooking Lunga Point, Jap artillery fired down on the invaders. There was no front, and there was no rear. It was an insane, mixed up mess of infiltration and murderous raids by both sides.

On August 20th the first big clash, between massed forces, exploded along the Tenaru River, not far into the jungle. So poor were the American maps that they did not know that the muddy stream actually was Alligator Creek, not the Tenaru River. But the name stuck to this first full-scale battle, only 3000 yards east of Henderson Field.

In black darkness, yammering machine guns, roaring explosions and thudding mortar bursts made a hell of the thickly overgrown mud banks, on each side Japs and Yanks smashed at each other with every weapon. Morning revealed over 900 dead Japs, as the defenders backed

38

away into the jungle. Hundreds of dead Americans lined the other bank of the gloomy little creek. Here the Army's 164th Regiment, fighting alongside the leathernecks, won a typical Marine title of praise—the nickname of "The 164th Army-Marines."

Pressing slowly ahead, the Marines met constantly advancing Jap reinforcements. Through the steaming muck, invisible from only a few yards away, little groups sought each other, grappled, and killed in gasping nightmare struggles. Marine Lieutenant Larry Hickson (Seattle, Washington), leading a crawling patrol, turned to call one of his men, who seemed to be too far off to one side. It was a Jap. Both fired almost at the same time. The Jap fell dead, hit in the heart, while a bullet smashed Hickson's arm. That was how it went in the cloudy ground haze on the 'Canal.

On one hilltop, Marines found a Jap flag flying from a post atop a hut. As they climbed up to remove the "meatball" ensign, an American plane dove down and bombed them, killing seven men. That was how things seemed to go on the accursed island.

It was well that the Americans had the will and guts to meet adversity. "Indian war" was the routine in the ever-damp, stinking jungle. Sudden ambush, sudden death —they were everyday, and every night. A shot, and the rustle of leaves; a knife flash and the gurgle of blood choking a slit throat—that was Guadalcanal.

Dysentery was everyone's curse—"the crud," they called it. Every half hour sick men, stomachs gripped by convulsive cramps, had to defecate. Many a man died in horrible ugliness and misery, shot or stabbed as he squatted to relieve himself.

Malaria and Dengue racked the men. Shaking with fever or chills, thin and wan, men who should have been on hospital beds slithered through the disease-filled mud. Many who were still in their teens looked like old men. Their skins were furrowed and cracked, and red-rimmed eyes stared vacantly from dark eye sockets. Many men lost forty or fifty pounds, and looked like living corpses.

Jungle rot—a leprous white or yellow rotten puffing— ate into the skin of almost every gyrene. Never dry, as

39

sweat soaked them in the sticky humidity, men literally rotted in the terrible, steaming, tropical heat.

Not far from the native village of Tassafaronga, on September 5th, two light tanks accompanying a Marine advance ran into the kind of fighting that was a synonym for Guadalcanal.

Out of hidden holes, swarms of Japs rose to meet the Marines, and machine guns sprayed so thickly through the undergrowth that clipped leaves and twigs rained down. Led by Lieutenant William Petoskey of Pittsburgh, Pennsylvania, the Marines charged with naked bayonets. Steel clashed with steel, as shrieking Nipponese dueled with the Americans, and the jungle echoed with screams of rage and fear. Then it quieted for a moment, to groans and horrible gurgling noises.

In one tank, Sergeant Ralph O'Connor (Boston, Mass.) raised his head to peer out, and got a bullet through his head. The tank bogged down in a mud hole, and the rest of its crew fought their way out against Japs who swarmed over them with knives and bayonets.

The other tank jammed between two trees. Suicidal Japs crawled up to it and drenched it with gasoline. While its Commander, Sergeant Dave Abramowitz (Jersey City, N.J.), fired its machine guns desperately, the Japs set the stuck tank afire. They actually beat on the tank's sides with fists and knives, screaming wildly. Abramowitz was stabbed to death as he climbed out of the tank, but the other crewmen had escaped under the cover of his machine gun. Later, thirty-eight dead Japs were counted under the sweep of the dead tank's gun.

Rain poured down almost daily, turning the already damp earth into a deep slime. On both sides of *Iron Bottom Channel,* on 'Canal and Tulagi, the fighting went on, and the misery grew endless. How men could rise to bursts of violent courage, in that sodden muck, is hard to understand.

Take Sergeant Jesse Glover, of the 6th Marines. He was on Gavutu, one of the many shore fringe islands. One morning he and his squad came upon a native hut, in a clearing. It was impossible to tell whether or not there were any Japs in it.

Glover, an "old pro" who called the Corps his home, quietly bawled out his squad for hesitating. Then he took some extra hand grenades and started towards the hut, all alone. Waiting at the edge of the clearing, the men saw him dash to the door of the hut. He kicked it open, and plunged inside.

As he disappeared into the hut they heard the crack of a grenade, and part of the straw hut blew out. Above the echoes they heard Glover's bull-throated voice bellowing joyously:

*"Good morning, you bastards!"*—Blam!
*"Good morning, you bastards!"*—Blam!
*"Good morning, you bastards!"*—Blam!

Each explosion, and the flying straw walls, told of Glover's passage from room to room of the hut. When his squad came up to join him, they found the sergeant happily surveying his work. He was unharmed, but in the reeking havoc of the hut lay the torn parts of nine Japanese soldiers.

But joyous carnage like that was not the rule of the dark and bloody islands. Especially on the big one, 'Canal, there was little laughter—except by the psychos, who sometimes broke down in insane cackling, as their minds gave way under the grisly horror. The men in the line don't ever laugh very much. They don't remember how.

Many men were hit and lost in the dense underbrush. Invisible from a few feet away, and unable or not daring to call for help, they gasped their lives out there. No one will ever know how many men, of both sides, died like stricken animals on Guadalcanal's tangled floor. Other men, like Lieutenant Jim Snell (Enid, Oklahoma), of Edson's Raiders, suddenly collapsed, overcome by heat and exhaustion, and lay helplessly paralyzed.

Only a few Jap civilian laborers surrendered. All other Japs preferred death to the shame of surrender. At Matanikaw, one of the coastal villages, Marines were test-firing a captured pom-pom gun, when suddenly a white flag appeared near the village. A group of terrified Nipponse laborers, who thought they were being fired on, came out to surrender. They were the only ones to give up, except stunned or helpless Japanese.

41

After a while, the atmosphere of killing destroyed all normal thoughts of mercy. One Marine saw six Japs come running toward him, apparently unarmed. Taking no chances, he opened up with a BAR, and cut them all down. Later, examination of the bodies revealed no weapons on them. Perhaps they were trying to surrender! No one will ever know.

More often, there were no doubts. A man would spot an enemy running, and the cry would go up, like the baying of hounds: "There he goes! Get the bastard! Kill the SOB!" Rapping rifle fire would follow the terrified Jap, cut him down, and then tear holes in his twitching body. Mercy was too dangerous, when "dead" or wounded Japs would suddenly come to life and attack corpsmen who stopped to bind up their wounds.

Many times the Marines found enemies holed up in caves, from which they emerged now and then to shoot and run. Here began the sickening task that was to continue all across the Pacific—the blasting shut of cave entrances with dynamite, sealing the inhabitants alive in their tombs. In one cave a wounded Jap officer was found still alive. An interpreter called to him to surrender. The answer was a grenade. And the last word was a satchel charge that sealed the cave mouth, entombing the fanatical officer. In another cave, three Japs were cornered. They had only one pistol, which they kept firing. The last three shots seemed to be inside the cave. Later, it was seen that they had used their last three bullets to kill themselves.

So it went on 'Canal, as the stench of disease, death, and rotting corpses turned the humid air to poison. The stink of Guadalcanal was something never to be forgotten. It was the smell of hell on earth.

Madness seized some men. Sergeant Angus Goss (Detroit, Michigan) had a hard time with one cave. Every grenade he pitched in came sailing back out. Then he pushed a satchel charge into the entrance. The Japs threw it out, near Goss. The explosion ripped the skin from his leg. Streaming with blood, and wholly maddened, Goss sprang to his feet. His tommy gun firing steadily, he leaped into the cave, spraying bullets into it. Eight Japs went down

42

before the hail of flying lead. Unharmed, Goss emerged from the cave, eyes blazing with fury. Questioned later, he said "I just got mad. Everything got red in front of my eyes. I had to kill those damn Japs."

Back on Henderson Field, the few available old Grumman Marine and Navy planes did unbelievable flying against new Zeros that could outspeed, outclimb and outmaneuver them. Just to refuel a plane took hours of labor, when gasoline had to be hand bailed out of fifty-five-gallon drums. Poor radios limited communications to a twenty-mile range. Flyers lived on cold Spam, like the GIs in the line. Even so, such great pilots as Captain Joe Foss were there, and they took a fearful toll of Jap planes.

On October 25th the Japs launched a massive attack in a desperate effort to smash the Americans. By then 30,000 Nipponese troops were available, and all of them were used. Failure to coordinate the assault on the flanks led to its failure. Fanatically brave, as ever, the Japs launched wave after wave of screaming Banzai attacks, led by sword swinging officers. Delayed and confused in the thick jungle, each wave struggled forward only to be cut to pieces by waiting Marine and Army units.

For two days and nights the attacks continued, only to be beaten back by the haggard, red-eyed Yanks. When the Americans were on the verge of exhaustion, almost unable to fight back, the attacks suddenly stopped. The Japanese had lost nearly 4000 men, and were retreating.

Dead bodies and bloody pools littered the murky jungle, like a scene from Dante's Inferno. Bodies rotting on the jungle floor bloated like overstuffed sausages, and burst, to emit a nauseating stench that hung like a cloud. Millions of maggots crawled over and in the dead bodies.

Again the grim advance resumed, and the blasting of caves of the holed-up enemy began again. Marine Captain Harold Torgerson (Valley Stream, New York) alone blasted forty caves. His method was to run to a cave mouth, while some of his men covered him. Then he would light his dynamite fuse, shove the charge into the hole, and run. Sometimes he tied gasoline cans to the charge "for added flavor." Once he was blown fifteen feet by one explosion, and his clothes were almost ripped off. Arising,

43

he remarked calmly "Boy, that was a beaut! Even better than 4th of July!"

Marine Sergeant Max Koplow (Toledo, Ohio), tangled with three Japs, killed one with one shot, and was seized by the others. Unable to point his gun, he used it as a club, and killed the other two with its butt. Then, as he lay panting, two more Japs leaped on him. In a brutal wrestling bout with them, while they stabbed at him with knives, he turned one attacker's knife against its owner, and killed him with it. Finally, one knee holding down his last enemy's knife hand, he strangled the Jap with his bare hands. Then he collapsed with eight knife wounds in his body.

Disease became rampant. Shattered Japanese food stores of canned fish stank horribly in the tropic heat. No latrines could be built, and the thousands of dysentery and malaria-racked men relieved themselves and vomited where they could. Nauseating mounds of human excrement were everywhere. All this, and rotting bodies, cooked and steamed in the fierce heat. A pestilential miasma of foulness covered everything.

In this sickening stench, swarms of flies traveled from fish to excrement, to maggoty corpses, and to food, as the men forced themselves to eat. Soon every man was haggard with fever, while medical stores ran out. Then food was cut down to one can of C Ration per day, as the *Tokyo Express* sank incoming supply ships. Few men tried to shave any longer. On all their grimy, deeply-lined, stubbled faces there was "the look" of soul-sick combat veterans.

Guadalcanal was all this. The island stank and reeked with ugliness, death, disease and horror. No nightmare of hell could possibly have been worse. Men who lived through it still grow silent and staring-eyed at the memory of that horrible, awful place.

After a time the men became dull-eyed, nearly numb killing-machines, almost beyond feeling or thought. The ultimate example was Private "Red" Van Orden (Oklahoma City, Oklahoma), of the 2nd Marines, aged 18 years. He and a buddy crawled slowly all one morning, to knock out a machine gun nest. Van Orden found it, and killed its crew of four, finishing the last one with a gun butt smash. Then, returning to his lines, he reported the incident to his CO. The officer, with wry irony, jokingly asked "Why didn't you bring back the machine gun?" The tired Marine listened seriously.

Numbly, Van Orden went out again, and returned a little later. Silently, he laid the Jap machine gun at the Captain's feet. Later, in January, the quiet young man was killed by a shell burst in the last drive to secure the island.

Curiously, after all the Marines' suffering, it was an Army Division that broke the back of the Japanese defense. At Mount Austen, which dominated Henderson Field, the American Division locked in massive lines of combat with the core of the defense force, early in December. Seven times the 132nd Infantry charged up the barren slopes. Seven times the crack Oka Regiment, defending the mountain, counterattacked. The GIs' last charge broke the defense line. From then on the Jap defeat was certain.

On December 16th, a 1st Marine night infiltration patrol found some sixty Japs quietly camped around a fire far behind the battle lines. Silently the patrol ringed the peaceful scene. At a signal from Lieutenant Claude Grout (Athens, Georgia) they all fired at once, killing every one of the stunned enemy. Then they moved in and shot the fallen Japs again—just to be sure. Minutes later the patrol moved on. Behind them the campfire still flickered, its lights and shadows dancing over the still bodies of sixty dead men. That was how death struck on "the 'Canal."

On another patrol, out of Edson's Raiders, a squad was hit by mortar fire, leaving only three men alive. One of them, his stomach torn open, and losing blood fast, was Private Ray Herndon (Walterboro, South Carolina). Knowing that he was dying, he told the others to go back, as they heard Japs slithering through the brush to finish them off. He propped his gun up, facing the enemy, and told the others: "You guys get out of here. I'm done for anyhow. I'll get some of the bastards before I pass out. Now scram!"

Early in December the malaria-ridden, staggering men of

45

the 1st Marines were relieved. Many were too weak to climb the nets to board the transports back to Lunga. Soon after, the 10th and 2nd Marines also were pulled out. They were so sick and exhausted that their combat value had become dangerously low. The Army's 25th and American Divisions went on with the dirty business.

It was to take a full year before the 1st Marine Division could again be brought back to fighting condition. The 2nd Marines, having had comparatively little fighting on Guadalcanal, were able to move out late in the year to the deadly Tarawa landings. There, in November, 1943, their brutal training at "the 'Canal" paid dividends.

In January and February the Army Divisions pressed forward to finish the miserable job. As days passed resistance became weak, though it flared up violently every once in a while. In the last days the big island became a grisly killing ground. Methodically, the GIs killed off the fanatical Japs, while the *Tokyo Express* struggled to evacuate the defeated Imperial Army. 11,000 Japs did escape, but nearly 30,000 were butchered when they stubbornly refused to surrender. By February the gloomy mud of the island was blood-soaked, from one end to the other. In mid-February it was over. Guadalcanal was secure. The blood-letting was done with.

With the taking of "the 'Canal," the march towards Tokyo and victory began. Counting the price, the leaders of the American fighting forces shook their heads gloomily. It was too costly. The fighting men said nothing, hardly believing that they were still alive.

Yet, very soon, the optimism that is so typical of the Yanks flared up again. If they had won through hell itself—and Guadalcanal was literally hell on earth—then what could stop them now? Nothing! And the Japanese knew that they could never win. If they had lost when hell itself fought for them, when could they ever win? Never!

So it happened, in fact. The men who served their time in hell, on Guadalcanal, had served for all the Americans. With their suffering they had brought the assurance of victory.

They looked back with haunted eyes at the terrible, un-

46

natural island, as on a nightmare. For the rest of their lives they would shudder inwardly when they heard the name of Guadalcanal.

Surely the men who sleep forever in the cemetery there deserve the pity and gratitude that no longer can reach them. But for the living, the name of that awful island always will mean one thing—the heartsick emotion of men facing death in a stinking hell—*Guadalcanal.*

# THE BLOODY SANDS OF NORMANDY

## By Kimble Stevens

UTAH, OMAHA, GOLD, JUNO, AND SWORD were their battle
names, the five red beaches of Normandy—scene of the
most terrific invasion of all time—*Operation Overlord*.
Once they were red with blood and fire. They always will
glow with the invisible red badges of courage.

Much has been said about the vast Normandy invasion. But the terrific drama on the five red beaches themselves has remained a confused mass of bits and pieces
of stories. Perhaps it was too vast and awesome to be
described as a single story. But it *was* a single story. A
story of thousands of men who gambled their lives on the
fire-swept sands. And of the thousands whose blood
stained the salt-streaked shores of France on June 6,
1944.

Utah Beach was the westernmost assault area. It lay
on the corner of the Contentin (Cherbourg) Peninsula,
around the swampy land of Varreville. Over it went the
82nd Airborne Division and the 101st Airborne Division,
dropping out of the sky around Ste. Mere Eglise. And to it
went the 4th Infantry Divison, part of the 90th Infantry
Division, and VII Corps.

Just to the east was Omaha Beach, separated from
Utah only by the Vire River and swamps around Isigny.
It stretched for three miles, from Grandcamp to Vier-
ville, to St. Laurent, and to Colleville. To it went the 1st
Infantry Division, the 29th Infantry Division, and V
Corps.

Next was Gold Beach, stretching from Port-en-Bessin to
past Arromanches. There the British 50th Division went
in.

Juno Beach followed, just to the east, around Cour-
seulles. To it went the 3rd Canadian Division.

Last, but far from least, was Sword Beach, from Lion-
sur-Mer to Ouistreham. There the British 6th Airborne
Division dropped across the Orne River, between Caen
and Cabourg. And to it went the British 3rd Division.

First U. S. Army Headquarters commanded the landings
of the American Divisons, on Utah and Omaha Beaches.
Second British Army Headquarters commanded the Eng-
lish and Canadian divisions, on Gold, Juno, and Sword
Beaches. By comparison with *Overlord,* and its assault
plan, Neptune, the greatest other amphibious landings in
Africa, Italy, southern France, Guadalcanal, Saipan,
Guam, Iwo Jima, and Okinawa were only small raids.
*Overlord* was *The* Big One.

Back on the English coast the Allied Supreme Commander General Dwight D. Eisenhower, stared into the
shadowy blackness, and prayed. Column after column of
silent men moved forward, past him, to the greatest seaborne assault in history. Once started, the huge force was
like a human tide, sweeping across the English Channel,
to crash onto the other shore.

In this one tremendous assault, the quiet anger of free
men against tyranny and oppression exploded in a terrific
burst of shattering violence. In it was concentrated the
combined will, determination and readiness to dare death
of multitudes of ordinary Americans, Canadians, and
Britons. On June 6, 1944, the Allied Nations-In-Arms
stormed the walls of Adolf Hitler's *Festung Europa,* and
in one blazing day of battle, smashed the shell of the
most frightful tyranny the world ever had seen.

First blood was drawn at 0130 on the night of June 5-6,
when paratroopers of the 101st Airborne dropped right
on top of a Regimental HQ of the German 709th Division
in St. Floxel, a village on the Cherbourg Peninsula. The
startled Germans woke to find themselves under tommy-
gun fire from the grim paratroopers. After that the night
became hideous for the Germans. All over the flanks of
the five-beach area, groups of tough paratroopers of the
101st and 82nd Divisions dropped from the skies. By

49

morning dozens of vicious little melees were swirling in the rear of the German Westwall defenses. At the same time, bands of French Resistance fighters began to cut German communications. The ways *out* of the beaches were temporarily opened, if the assault landings should be successful.

Air assault began at dawn. But luck was against the bombers. Heavy overcast made it necessary to bomb the coastal forts by instruments. Of 13,000 bombs dropped by 329 B-24 bombers on Omaha Beach, for example, not one hit the beach defenses. Instead they struck two or three miles beyond. Later, this seeming misfortune was to turn out to be a blessing in disguise.

At Utah Beach medium bombers attacked visually, with better results. Two-thirds of the bombs hit the beach. Of 360 bombers, 293 hit the defenses there, while 67 did not release their bombs because of the thick overcast.

All in all, the air bombardment did not weaken the beach defenses greatly. Grey, opaque haze saved the German coastal forts from the racing swarms of planes. But it also hid the approach of the huge invasion fleet, which was far more important. On a clear day, the planes could have inflicted some damage on enemy guns, but some would have remained to do *their* dirty work.

In the channel, Allied fighting ships drove off a few German torpedo boats that vainly tried to attack the great Armada. Heavy seas made it impossible for the little boats to return to the attack.

As first light dawned, rows of Allied battleships, cruisers and destroyers ranged up and down the invasion coast. Thundering salvos of big gun fire hurled huge projectiles over the heads of packed troop-carriers and landing craft. Then rocket-firing ships blasted the beaches just before the landing craft reached shore.

Again the softening-up fire was ineffective. Most of the German fortifications were well-concealed against fire from the sea. Most of the rockets overshot the beach, to explode harmlessly on higher ground.

Yet, both the air and sea bombardment had highly important (and quite unexpected) results. The bombing detonated large minefields between defensive strong points, and saved the invaders from many casualties. After the landings, naval gunfire was to be invaluable in knocking out key strong points. Air attack and strafing repeatedly broke up enemy concentrations, and barred reinforcements from moving swiftly to the beach defenses. And most important, it kept the Luftwaffe off the necks of the harassed foot soldiers.

Ninth Air Force fighters and bombers, alone, flew almost three thousand tactical missions that day, in the American zone. Against them the Luftwaffe sent five hundred sorties. Far beyond the battle area the American planes tangled with the Germans in a wild series of duels. Hardly a single German plane reached the beaches.

As dawn broke through the grey, murky haze, the landing craft wallowed heavily toward the five red beaches. German coastal batteries, alerted by the air and naval bombardment, were beginning to thud up and down the coast. It had begun.

Most fortunate of all were the men assigned to the westernmost beach. Luck smiled on them. Swamps behind the flat beaches had caused the Germans to discount this area as a possible route of invasion. Just beyond the wide, sandy beaches, heavy bogs seemed to bar exit. Only four narrow causeways crossed the swamps. Beyond them, soon enough, there would be powerful defenses. But the beaches themselves were only lightly defended.

Fourth Division men formed the assault wave. In the very first wave rode Brig. Gen. Theodore Roosevelt, Jr., famous son of a famous father. As Assistant Division Commander he could have waited on a safe transport, at Division HQ. Instead he came in like any GI, to help organize the attack inland. Generals who actually lead —from in front—are rare today. But danger is the price of valor. This brave battle leader was to be killed in action soon after.

Billowing smoke and dust on the shore at Varreville blinded the plunging little LCVP's, and strong currents pulled them far south. Lucky for them, too. Booming cannon and snarling machine guns spat through the blinding murk. An LCT loaded with four DD tanks struck a mine there, and sank near the shore. Another control ship was torn apart by a heaving geyser exploded by a mine. But the landing craft bored in.

On the little St. Marcouf Islands there, 4th and 24th Cavalry Squadron men landed, to clear the flank of the beach. Artillery fire from inland burst among the running Yanks, and mines erupted under their feet. Pieces of men flew through the roaring air, and blood stained the yellow sand. But it was not as bad as had been expected. Only nineteen casualties out of the 132 detachment was cheap, in terms of battle advantage. They took the crucial little islands, fast.

Swept almost a mile south by the currents, the first wave touched down on a deserted stretch of beach, near the tiny village of La Grande Dune. Running waves of Infantry moved heavily up the soft sands, and disappeared into the thick swamp grass beyond.

Chattering machine guns barked sporadically. Here and there a running GI pitched forward, then lay still. Spots of blood sank quickly into the powdery sand. Lines of soldiers moved steadily across the beach, ignoring the scattered, huddled figures lying so quietly on the sand. The machine guns had to be silenced, before any thought could be given to the wounded or dead.

Fierce bursts of tommy gun fire and the flat whacking of M-1 shots spanged above the ripping sound of the German fire. Then the quick, tearing sounds stopped.

In minutes it was over. The beach was taken.

An hour after the first wave had hit the beach, routine landings were under way. One after another the landing craft touched down and disgorged their human cargos. Engineers swept the area for mines, cleared lanes, and blew gaps in a low seawall beyond the beach.

From inland, shells rumbled down, to burst here and there on the wide beach. In quiet, matter-of-fact order, the buildup went on, ignoring the occasional roaring bursts of shell explosions. Long lines of GIs trudged up the beach and disappeared into the grassy swamp area.

Every now and then a shellburst struck near a line of moving men. A roar, a hiss of flying shards, and the gasping of wounded men as blood poured from holes torn in their bodies. Quickly, first aid men bent over the wounded, to stop the bleeding, and take them back. Sometimes they stuck a rifle muzzle down in the sand, alongside a dead man. Later the burial details would find them. Two hundred men of the 4th Division fell before the day ended.

And the lines of men moved on—up the sand and forward. Men of the 4th and 90th Division.

Utah Beach was taken. It had been technically "easy" except to the drowned, wounded, and dead.

All the bloody havoc that had been feared did happen —on Omaha, the scarlet center of the five red beaches.

First Division and 29th Division Regiments stormed this key sector, at fearful cost. A shallow beach, backed by steep bluffs up to 170 feet high and intricate defense works, faced the invaders. Frowning capes towered over loose stone shingle and sand shopes, piled up to seawalls and embankments in a three-mile crescent. Five steep draws led out of the rough beaches. The only exits, they were heavily fortified by the Germans.

Thirty-six DD tanks of the 741st Tank Battalion led the assault lines toward the shore. Towering waves and crashing surf engulfed them, before they even neared the beach. All but five sank beneath the foaming waters, dragging their crews down to choking death.

Ten miles out, the packed transports unloaded their men, in darkness, into pitching LCVP's. Rolling combers swept into the troop carrier craft, swamping many of them. Fifteen big, crowded landing craft sank with their heavily burdened human cargos. Many a fighting man never saw the beaches to which he had come so long a way.

Helpless soldiers, hardly able to stand under their burdens of weapons and equipment, saw one craft after another sink from view. Artillery-carrying DUKW's were almost all buried beneath the frothing combers. Only one howitzer of the entire 111th Field Artillery Battalion reached shore. Most of the 7th F. A. Battalion's 105's were lost. Only one howitzer of a whole Cannon Company made it. Half the 58th Armored F. A. Battalion almost reached shore, only to be blasted by exploding mines. There would be no artillery to tear a way out from the beach.

Hundreds of Americans drowned far from the shore, unseen and unaided in their helplessness. Still the laboring LCVP's wallowed forward. As they neared the beaches, machine gun bullets drummed against the steel sides and ramps of their craft, and whipped the water into froth.

Unknown to Allied intelligence agents, a whole crack German Infantry Division had been on maneuvers at Omaha Beach—the 352nd Division. Elite, picked German troops manned the defenses, with every advantage of position, fortifications, and luck. They would have been tough enough enemies in even combat. To smash through them in frontal assault from a rough sea was a brutally hard job.

But there could be no turning back. The landing craft came on—into the grinning stone and steel face of death.

Over a hundred yards from shore the LCVP's dropped their ramps. Streams of bullets poured into the open craft. As men poised on the ramps, ready to leap into the neck-deep water, they spun around, blood spurting from bullet holes in chest, neck, face or head, and pitched down into the sea. In one craft a direct shell hit struck the packed men. In one blasting flash they were converted into a ghastly shambles of flesh and bones. Blood ran in streams along the floor, to pour in a dark cascade down the ramp, and to redden the green waters.

Neck deep, and holding their rifles over heads, the GI's waded laboriously toward the shore. Here and there a man dropped from sight as a bullet crashed into his brain. A few stopped to rest behind jutting obstacles, or alongside careened landing craft. Others fell exhausted at the water's edge. And overall a roaring inferno of bullets and shells screamed and bellowed.

At Vierville draw, Rangers in two LCVP's met shattering fire. One craft sank and the other was torn by hit after hit from big mortars up on the bluffs. Machine guns raked the survivors as they staggered up the beach. A trail of bloodstains and sprawled bodies marked the path of the few who managed to reach the shelter of the seawall. Infantry carriers with them met the same fate. Bloody death reigned at Vierville. The 116th Infantry was almost wiped out there. It was a bad time for the 1st Division.

Eddying smoke and dust clouded the bluffs as the men struggled ashore all up and down the deadly beach. Behind the beach German guns, zeroed-in long before, raked the open sands. The smoke hid the defenders from the panting, half-shattered attackers. Six tanks out of eighteen got to shore at Vierville. Then, blinded by smoke and dust, they ground heavily along, their big guns smashing in baffled rage at the towering bluffs above.

It was the same at Colleville and St. Laurent. Bodies sprawled grotesquely in the sand. Many lay half buried, while the oblivious surf rolled and slid along or over them. White-faced survivors panted behind the rough seawall. A few tanks, all that were left of the battalion that had started for shore, bellowed futilely at the frowning bluffs. Scattered, mixed-up remnants of units cowered in confused clumps of shocked, exhausted men.

The shattered 116th Infantry's position was typical. Its Command Craft was smashed with all its officers and men. Most of the Company and Platoon Leaders were killed right at the beginning. Only a few of its radios were left in operation. Sixty percent of its Engineers, vitally needed to clear paths through minefields, lay sprawled in death. And almost all its minefield clearing and marking equipment was lost. Offshore, confused LCT's were milling around uncertainly, while bursting shells whacked over and around them. It looked like utter disaster. A red haze seemed to hang over the death-filled beach, while patches of blood turned darker under a drifting grey pall.

Up on the bluff the German Fortress Commander grunted with satisfaction. The *Verdamte Amerikaner* were being butchered. He sent a message off to his head-quarters, to Von Rundstedt and Rommel. "American invasion is stopped on the beaches. Heavy losses being inflicted on survivors. Burning vehicles and dead and wounded Americans litter the beaches. Heil Hitler."

But he spoke too soon. The Americans were not beaten yet. Offshore, in a wallowing DUKW, Col. Benjamin B. Talley, Asst. Chief of Staff of V Corps, radioed back to Generals Gerow and Bradley. The situation called for action. First Army HQ replied, "Send in the next waves!" More lines of landing craft came lurching and plunging towards the shore.

Meanwhile, among the scattered, confused groups on the shore, the first shock was wearing off. Uproar, blasting geysers of fire, blood and death were becoming familiar and not quite so terrifying. Long training protected the men as they sheltered themselves from the screaming hail of flying steel. Intrepid men took command of what was left of companies and battalions and started upslope, toward the enemy. Lieutenants, sergeants and corporals rose to lead, and the infantrymen began to follow, in little groups.

Second Lt. John M. Spalding led twenty men, all that was left of G Company, 16th Infantry, up the draw at St. Laurent. Yankee machine guns and mortars on the beach began to spit defiantly. Spalding's group topped the bluff. From behind, they attacked the pillboxes and forts with grenades and satchel charges. Terrified Germans resisted for a while, then surrendered.

At Colleville, Sgt. Philip Tucker led four men up the side of a cliff, to grenade a pillbox and gun down a machine gun crew that tried to run.

At Pointe du Hoe, Lt. Col. James E. Rudder led the 2nd Rangers ashore under point-blank covering fire by destroyers near the beach. With scaling ladders the Rangers swarmed up the cliffs, while shells burst against the cliff wall and rim. Streaming with blood from first one wound and then a second, Rudder led his men over the cliff. Beyond it German Artillery crews ran, leaving their big 155's deserted.

At Vierville, PFC Milton Levine led six 1st Division

56

Rangers up the fire-swept draw. One by one the men were hit and killed by machine gun fire from the edges of the draw. With one other man Levine crawled to the top of the rim. His last partner was killed by a burst as they came up to the machine gun nest.

Rising to one knee, Levine fired shot after shot from his rifle, killing the crew while they tried to bring the machine gun to bear on him. Then he ran to the weapon, swung it around, and riddled the crew of another German machine gun nest nearby.

As these and other stabbing thrusts pierced the defense line, the German division began to weaken. Pounding fire from naval guns began to smash the fortifications. At the Les Moulins draw, the 116th Infantry and 5th Rangers drove through the defenses, and punched two hundred yards inland.

Thirty-seventh and 146th Engineer Combat Battalions bulldozed gaps over the ditches, and cleared the minefields at St. Laurent draw. Close-up destroyer fire from the sea punched out one pillbox after another. At noon the German unit there surrendered to the 18th Infantry.

By afternoon the filtering spearheads of advance had become wedges, and then columns. Frightened German veterans backed away from these Americans who started to fight when they should have been finished. As dusk fell, the beachhead had expanded well past the deadly bluffs. The first of the build-up forces, the 26th Division, was coming ashore in orderly columns.

It was over. Omaha Beach was taken. From one end of the great crescent to the other bodies lay sprawled, amid shattered vehicles and landing craft. From the edge of the plateau above, the long beach seemed to be spattered with dull red dots next to huddled, broken dolls. But the beach was secure. That was Omaha, bloodiest of the five bloody beaches.

The British 50th Division came in like its American Allies on its right, in wallowing landing craft. Luck was with the Limeys on the first day. After that they were to have a "rough go." The Germans did not fight hard on this beach. They had other plans—to let the invaders come ashore and then pound them to pieces as they tried to move up the slopes toward Bayeux and Caen.

Craggy, broken beaches in this area had seemed to the Germans to be altogether unsuited for assault from the sea. And the British landings luckily hit just the weakest part of the defenses, between Le Hamel and La Riviere. Second-rate German Occupation Troops broke and fled from the attack of the vengeful Englishmen.

Driving assault by the 47th Royal Marine Commandos took its light losses, and stormed quickly over the beaches. Only a few dozen men fell under the enemy fire, to mark the sand with the inevitable red stains.

Against light resistance the English Division drove swiftly ashore. By evening its outposts were over five miles inland, nearing Bayeux. It was to be a miserably tough deadlock above Caen, only a few hours later, but that's another story.

Like its right flank neighbor, the 3rd Canadian Division landed almost unopposed, above Courselles. It, too, hit an almost undefended beach. And second-string German Occupation Troops broke on first contact with the tough Canadians.

In swift advance, the division's spearheads had moved five miles inland by evening, while armored patrols were feeling their way another two miles ahead.

Nearly three hundred Canadians were hit on the beach near Courselles. Red stains marked that strip of sand. A German strong point held them on the beach until a destroyer punched it out with direct cannon fire from the sea. The Canucks would bleed worse, later, in the stalemate above Caen.

On the left flank beach, between Lion-sur-Mer and Ouistreham, the British 3rd Division led the way ashore. In the hours before dawn the British 6th Ariborne Division had dropped from the skies, out to the east. Like their Yankee counterparts on the other flanks, the English paratroopers raised general hell in the German back areas. They had much to revenge—four years of German murders of English men, women and children.

On the beach the landing craft ran directly at a German strong point. Almost two hundred Britons fell there, in a savage, close-up fight that left many red patches on the sand. There was more weeping soon on the great island across the channel. But the dogged men of England drove quickly on, past the beaches.

By evening they were five miles inland, and their advance patrols were threatening Caen. It was to be a long, grim struggle after that. Caen was the key to the German defense of Normandy. The Germans were to fight bitterly to hold it. But as June 6th ended, the British were solidly and safely ashore, in a roomy, solid beachhead they were to expand.

As dusk deepened at the end of that fateful day, the five beaches lay cloaked in fire-streaked darkness. On each one there lay wounded, moaning men—a few on some beaches, terribly many on one.

Across the sands, columns of fighting men trudged forward, toward the flame. The fight to liberate a continent in bondage had just begun. It would not end until the last would-be German slaveholder had bowed in abject defeat.

There was a long, bitter way to go. But the gates were opened—five sandy gates, spotted with red. Through them were pouring the grim Armies of Liberation.

A thousand years from now men will come to the five desolate beaches to stare and to wonder. They will remember and cherish the memory of the simple, gallant men whose blood carmined these sands.

Not all the winds nor rains nor tides of time can ever quite wash those spots away. The blood that made them has long since disappeared. Yet the marks will glow forever for all those who have hearts to see with.

# ANZIO'S MOST TORTURED DECISION: SHOULD WE KILL OUR OWN TROOPS?

### By Major Howard L. Oleck

ERNIE HARMON was a stocky, bull-muscled man. His close-clipped, iron-grey hair topped a massive, solid face. In the thrust of his stubborn jaw there was the firm decision of a man long accustomed to command. He was a professional soldier—American style.

"Old Gravel Voice" his men called him, because of his rough, harsh-sounding speech. But there was respect and affection in that nickname. "Old Gravel Voice" was rough and he was tough, but he was all man. And often he had shown an inner gentleness that his brusque manner belied. The men who followed his commands did so with deep faith and trust. In Morocco, Tunisia, and Salerno he had led them from victory to victory. If "Old Gravel Voice" said "Go," they went, without hesitation or doubts.

Major General Ernest N. Harmon had an impossible choice to make one rainy night in the dismal mud of Anzio Beachhead. Fate challenged him with a deadly riddle, and he had to gamble. This was no mere theoretical problem. It was "for keeps." Time for thought was short, and the stakes were high—almost 600 American lives.

Harmon was then the commander of the crack 1st Armored Division. Trapped in the blazing Anzio beachhead, in February 1944, the American and British units there had to make a stab at breaking out. Soon mud and rain would lock the opposing forces into a long stalemate. On the other side, the Germans were just as anxious to smash the beachhead, before it became too strong to be destroyed.

For the breakout attack, a special task force had gathered, by order of Major General John P. Lucas, commander of the Anzio invasion force, U. S. VI Corps. *Task Force Harmon* consisted of the 30th Infantry Regiment of the 3rd Infantry Division, half of the 6th Armored Infantry Regiment, two companies of tanks from the 1st Armored Regiment, and two full battalions of artillery from Harmon's division. It amounted to a large infantry force, with tanks and very heavy artillery support. Spearhead of the attack was to be the 30th Infantry.

For the assault, the plan was to blast a path for the GIs with terrific artillery fire. Then the infantry would push through, with close support from the tanks. It was bound to be tough, because a crack Nazi S. S. Division held the attack area. The fanatical S. S. troops, handpicked for the job, had the added advantages of higher defensive ground and deep mud, which would slow the attackers.

The irony of the situation was that the Germans had picked the same night, February 18th, to launch their own attack. Both sides were busy gathering assault forces.

At three o'clock in the morning the tired, soaked dogfaces were nearing the assembly area. With them came General Harmon, riding in an open jeep, rain pelting his face. Now and then he spoke over his radio, checking on the movement of the gathering units.

Just as they reached the rendezvous spot, Harmon's radio crackled with a sudden urgency. A German attack had begun, far behind them, on the other side of the beachhead perimeter. His infantry was needed back there, to strengthen the Allied line. Problem number one faced him. What should he do? Before the night was over this problem was to fade into insignificance, before another and much more torturous delemma. But a decision had to be made on *this* question, and it had to be made quickly.

Over their radios Harmon and Lucas spoke quickly.

"We need all the troops possible, right here," Lucas explained. "Can't tell yet how big an attack the Krauts are making here.We should not take unnecessary chances."

"It is better to keep them here," Harmon argued, his mind racing, calculating distances, march speeds, and a dozen other factors. "First of all, the men have been hiking all night. They are tired, and need rest. If they turn back now, they will be exhausted when they reach you. They will not be fit for action, after sixteen miles of night marching in mud and rain. Certainly they cannot reach you at all until morning."

Lucas listened, and then agreed. "Okay. Keep them where you are, and go on with your attack. At least they can get some rest before you move out. We can hold here with the troops we have."

The attack would go on as planned. Harmon called his artillery commander. Artillery was the key element in the assault plan. Two full artillery battalions were being readied for the barrage, the 27th and 91st Battalions.

A ladder barrage was the main feature of the artillery's job. In the chosen lane of attack, every enemy defensive area was to be plastered with terrific artillery bombardment. The whole path of attack was to be smashed and pulverized with high explosives. Every inch of that area was to be raked and ripped by the big guns.

Firing in box areas, one box after another, the artillery was to aim by map coordinates, blind. As each box was saturated, the guns would move up to the next box, and then the next, in step ladder order.

"The key to the whole atack is the *ladder barrage,*" Harmon emphasized once again to his artillery commander. "The path of attack must be absolutely swept clear of troops. There should be nothing left alive in that area. Even then my infantry will have a tough enough time with strong enemy forces on both flanks. That's an S. S. Division in front of us. When I tell you to commence firing, I want that attack area really clobbered. If the barrage is not effective the infantry will be slaughtered."

"Roger, sir. Wilco. Whenever you are ready," answered the gunnery officer. "We also will lead the attacking force with a curtain barrage when the infantry jumps off, as you ordered."

"Correct," Harmon concluded. "When I give the word, start the ladder barrage, and keep it going at ten-minute intervals, until dawn. That is when the infantry will start the assault. That is all, for now. Over and out."

It was nearly four o'clock in the morning. In about two hours daylight would appear. There was just enough time for the infantry to deploy in attack formation before them. Files of silent men turned towards their appointed jump-off spots. In a few minutes the barrage should be ordered to begin.

Suddenly the radio next to him snapped and crackled sharply. His call signals sounded urgently. The radioman next to him answered the call letters, and then listened attentively, holding the headphones to his ears.

"Urgent call for you, sir," he said to the general. "Emergency call from the 45th Infantry Headquarters. A Colonel Knox. It's about one of the 45th Division's units."

"What the deuce can they want," the general muttered.

"Harmon here. Yes, Colonel Knox. What's your trouble? We are about to start barrage."

Controlled excitement sounded in the voice of the man who was calling. "We know about your barrage, sir. That is why we are calling. Please hold your barrage. I say again. Please do not start your barrage. One of our infantry battalions is reported to be in the area of your barrage. Please do not begin firing."

Old Gravel Voice exploded with wrath. "What the devil do you mean—one of your battalions is in our barrage area? All units were told of this attack. What in tarnation are your people doing, interfering with this attack? Why didn't you get them out before this?"

"I'm very sorry, sir. We do not want to interfere. One of our battalions apparently got its directions mixed up, and took position right in the path of your attack. We are trying to contact them, to get them out. We thought we had moved all of our units out of the area. We had thought that it was all clear for you, until we got this report just now."

Anger, concern, and stabbing doubts racked the grey-

63

haired general. "This attack is vital, Colonel Knox. You know that. If we postpone it, the whole beachhead is endangered. General Lucas confirmed his order to launch the attack, just a little while ago. Orders are orders. The attack must go on. I cannot hold off the barrage for very long. How much time do you need?"

"Give us just a few minutes, sir," pleaded the 45th Division Officer. "We are trying to contact them now."

"All right," barked the old commander. "Call me in five minutes. We cannot wait much longer."

Calculations spun through his mind. He glanced at his wrist watch. 4:35. Dawn would break in less than two hours. Even if the ladder barrage began at once, it would only just barely saturate the target area, firing at ten minute intervals. It was too late to change the firing plan. An attempt to do so might make a futile mess of the whole plan. He had to decide, soon.

"One battalion of American infantry," he mused. "Almost six hundred young Americans—fathers of children, husbands, sons—six hundred. How can I order them to be destroyed by our own guns!"

"But what if you don't!" The faint, cold voice of duty answered. "The attack must be launched. If it isn't, maybe all of us will die. It's touch and go, right now. The Germans may drive us into the sea if we don't hit them, now, hard."

His mind rebelled. Attack with *no* artillery preparation! That was madness. The Krauts would slaughter infantry trying to attack upslope, without artillery, against intact defenses. To attack without a preparatory barrage meant to sacrifice perhaps thousands of GIs, not only six hundred.

The awful delemma of command! How often they had talked about it, in peacetime days. How smug and self-assured their opinions had been! Well, this was no theoretical problem. It was real, deadly real.

The radio crackled again. He snatched the earphones. "Harmon here. Yes, yes. What have you heard?"

Colonel Knox's voice sounded in his ears. It seemed to be a little less strained than before. "It's not quite as bad as we thought, sir. The unit in the barrage area is not a battalion. It's a single platoon."

Gratefully, Harmon nodded, still listening. A platoon —about forty men. That was a lot better than six hundred.

The Colonel's voice continued. "We have contacted them by radio. They have been ordered to get out of there as fast as they can. They are moving now, on their way. Thank you for waiting, sir. We cannot ask you to wait any longer, sir. Thanks for waiting this long."

"All right, Colonel. Glad you could reach them." Almost absently, Harmon put down the earphones. Forty men, not six hundred.

One platoon. Forty men. His lips tightened. That settled it. Without the barrage, his infantry would surely lose thousands of men. It was forty or thousands! Grimly, he nodded to the waiting radioman. "Call Artillery."

He glanced at his watch again. 4:52. Where had the minutes gone? He breathed deeply, then spoke:

"Commence firing."

As though his voice had echoed through the black night, ear-splitting thunder cracked forth in obedience, all around them. Deep in the dark shadows, emplaced gun muzzles spat sheets of flame into the night. Huge projectiles rumbled out over the rain-soaked blackness, hurtling towards the attack area.

Up ahead of them, geysers of flame leaped suddenly, in the assault zone, and danced fitfully. Flickering flashes, faintly seen, told of bursting shells, ripping and smashing, clearing path for the assault.

"God forgive me!" the general said softly to himself. "Forty men. God forgive me! It had to be done."

Through the driving rain, lines of men moved forward. The attack had begun.

Fate smiled on Harmon's choice. His resolute decision was the right one—more than right. It was a piece of extraordinary good fortune, for the Americans.

The lost 45th Division platoon escaped destruction. It turned out that contact had been established in the nick of time. Before the deadly barrage crashed into the target zone, the entire platoon moved out. It returned

65

safely to the American lines, without the loss of a man.

The Germans were preparing to launch their decisive bid for victory, at the very time that the Americans were doing the same thing. Their attack far on the other side of the beachhead perimeter had been only a feint. It was intended to deceive the Americans, and to draw troops away to that area. Harmon's decision *not* to send his infantry back, had defeated the German plan.

The real German attack was aimed at the Padiglione area—*exactly the same place where the Yanks were launching their attack*. Concentrated masses of German troops had gathered during the night, right in the middle of Harmon's ladder barrage target area. By some miracle the lost 45th Division platoon had passed right through the enemy staging area, unscathed and undetected.

As the lost platoon moved out of the target area, masses of picked Nazi infantrymen had moved into it. The ladder barrage zone was packed with waiting enemy troops, completely hidden in the darkness and rain. They too were going to attack at dawn.

Instead, the totally unexpected American ladder barrage fell suddenly, like thunderbolts, right onto the German troop masses. Boxed in by tremendous squares of exploding shells, the Nazis were smashed into a bloody shambles. Out of the black sky, a saturating rain of explosives ripped and tore the crowded grey ranks. The entire attack force was exterminated by the terrific bombardment. It was one of the most ghastily incidents of the entire war, from the German point of view.

At dawn the Americans moved forward, in their attack, against practically no opposition. Advancing GIs were amazed to find the area littered with dead and dying Germans. One GI remarked, "It looked like some insane slaughter house. Bodies, blood, and pieces of men were scattered all over the area. It was pretty horrible, but I was glad that it happened to them, rather than to us."

Beyond the ladder barrage area, strong defenses halted the advancing Yanks. The breakout had to wait, after all. But the German bid to destroy the beachhead had been smashed before it could be launched.

News of the extraordinary incident soon reached General Lucas, the beachhead commander, and Lt. Gen. Mark W. Clark, C.G. of U. S. Fifth Army. Congratulations poured in to the surprised Harmon's command post. His tortured decision had saved the Allies from a possible debacle. It had turned a very precarious beachhead into a secure springboard for the final Allied advance to Rome. Decorations and praise were rained on the slightly bewildered general. He could not see what all the fuss was about.

"A man must do what is right," he remarked, "and he should not expect praise for doing what has to be done. If the decision is hard, that is part of the job."

# THE FROGMEN OF ENIWETOK

### By David Gould
### Former CPO, USN

HE ROLLED to the edge of the rubber boat. Spray streamed against his face and side as the boat bounced and skipped on the black water. The muffled roar of the P.T. boat's engine blended with the rushing sound of wind.

"Gould next! Get set! . . ."

"Ready, now! *Go!*"

Water crashed against his shoulder as he dropped over the side. The dull throbbing of the engine disappeared quickly. The water was warm and pleasant. Low above the gently rolling waves the dim outline of the island loomed blackly out of the moonlit night. He started towards it, swimming slowly and easily.

So this was Eniwetok! The heavy "45" strapped to his hip, and the graph paper mapping board tied to his left thigh bothered him a little. He kept thinking of the cyanide capsule in his belt. "If about to be captured, break the capsule in your teeth. Death will be quick and painless"—that's what his training manuals had said.

It just didn't seem real. Here he was swimming towards an island occupied by Japanese who would kill him joyfully, if they could. Somewhere off to both sides of him in the dark ocean other men like him were swimming too—other *frogmen*—heading for the ominous island.

A sardonic smile creased his lean face for a moment. He was thinking back as he swam steadily shoreward. The daring *volunteers* who were "frogmen?" Volunteer, like *hell!* He had become a frogman in the old, old way of armies and navies: "We need volunteers. *You, you,* and *you!*" That was how *he* had *volunteered—by request.*

Long ago, quite unconscious of what it might portend, he had filled out a long classification card. When he joined the Navy, Dave Gould had requested Seabee duty. Logically, too. He was a metalworker, skilled in heavy metal construction and fabrication. So he had been made a Shipfitter First Class! That was typical of the military system, he thought.

But the classification card had had a blank headed by the word "Hobbies." So he had written in: "Swimming." Raised near the thundering surf of Long Island, he had grown up at the ocean's edge—learned to swim like a fish in the booming surf at Far Rockaway. Oh, he could swim well all right, easily and powerfully, in the roughest seas.

That's why he was where he was, swimming in shark infested Pacific Ocean waters, towards a deadly hostile island, in the night.

Suddenly, long ago, he had been sent by the Navy to Marine Boot Camp, and then to Underwater Demolitions School, in California. Bewildered, he had been taught to fight hand-to-hand, by tough Marine Drill Instructors. He had learned all the battle guile and fierce aggressiveness of the Marines. Then back to pure Navy, again, at U.D. School.

This first approach to Eniwetok was the easiest part, he thought idly, as he neared the dark bulk of the island. It would be six weeks yet before the vast invasion force hit the beaches here. He and the other men of his Underwater Demolitions Team had to prepare and clear the way for the Marines and G.I.'s who would storm this enemy sea fortress. He would be here again, himself, about ten days before the invasion. Then a third time, on the night before D-Day, too. And then hit the beach with the assault wave on D-Day itself.

"A nice assignment, this U.D.T. work!" he thought sarcastically.

About 100 yards offshore, he stopped swimming. Treading water, he rode the swells just outside the line where the breakers foamed over the outer coral reef. Only his head above water, he studied the shadowy beach. He could see surprisingly well in the moonlight. If there were sentries or guard posts along his sector of the shore, they were well concealed.

He swam to the edge of the reef, and gingerly paddled across it. When the assault wave hit it, the tide would be high enough to let the landing boats ride over the reef. He made a mental note of that fact. It was important—a matter of life or death for many men whom he never would know.

Hissing of low surf rolling onto the beach mingled with the whisper of a soft breeze and faint rustling of palm branches beyond the sandy beach. It would have been a fascinating, romantic night, in peacetime, he thought.

He pulled the graph paper clipboard off his leg, and snapped it onto his left arm. Took a grease pencil from his sheath, and began to make marks on his map. There, under a palm frond, a squat square outline told of a pillbox. He marked its position on his map.

There, off to the right a bit, a roundish mound indicated a gun pit. He moved a little closer. A long gun barrel jutted over it, close to the ground. Nearby were other emplacements, probably for machine guns, to sweep the beach. He marked them carefully on his map. The preinvasion aerial bombardment would take more than ample care of them.

Carefully he swam and waded back and forth across his beach sector. Ominous mines bobbed in the water, their horns ready to set off a blast on contact. Metal boat traps loomed silently under the shallows. Trip wires etched faint lines along the sand. Each was marked quickly and carefully on his map.

Once, a crouching noise on the beach froze him into icy rigidity. A figure was coming along the beach—then another. He crouched in the warm shallows. Two Japanese sentries went by. He could hear them talking casually as they went by. That had been close!

His wristwatch showed three o'clock. Time to start back. If he missed the pickup boat, that would be just too bad

70

*for him*. That was why he had been given the cyanide capsule.

If he missed the pickup, the boat probably could not risk another run to search for him in the darkness. That might tip off the whole invasion approach. If he "missed the boat," the choices left for him were simple and plain. He could swim out to sea until the sharks or squid got him. Or he could swim ashore and try to survive like an animal in the bush. That was damn unlikely on a small island like Eniwetok. No place to hide!

Surrender to the Japs was ruled out. They would torture the facts out of him, and slaughter the invaders when the Americans stormed ashore. So—the cyanide capsule! "Doesn't hurt a bit!" he thought grimly. "Well, the hell with that! Let's make the pickup!" He swam steadily away.

It was nearly dawn when he reached the pickup line, over a mile away from the beach. He could see the heads of other men of the U.D.T. detachment bobbing in the water. He took his place in the strung out line, and waited.

Out of the grey-blackness the P.T. boat came rushing towards them. As it came near he could see the pickup man seated on the bow of the pickup boat. A heavy leather loop was swung around his shoulder and trailed down over the side.

As the boat neared him, rushing along at nearly 30 knots, he raised one arm over his head, elbow bent. The loop would catch his rigid arm, yank him up, and pitch him bodily into the boat as it went by. It all depended on Jim Purvis, the big pickup man, to catch him like a fish, and swing him aboard the speeding boat.

*"Whack"*

His arm seemed to be pulled by a giant force, almost wrenched off his shoulder. The loop had caught. He was pulled flat, breathlessly. Then flung through the air in an arc, to crash down against the padded side of the boat. He lay there for a moment, half stunned. Then clambered quickly back, to make room for the next man to be flung aboard.

"Visit number one is nearly over—thank the Lord!"

71

he thought to himself. The boat turned and rushed out to sea, towards the destroyer escort that waited for them. There the Intelligence officers would take his maps, and question him as to what he had seen.

He relaxed slowly. "Nice night for a swim," he said to the wet, tired man next to him.

Four weeks later, on another bright moonlit night, Dave Gould was swimming in at the beach on Eniwetok again. This was no mere reconnaissance trip, this time. He was heavily burden with blocks of explosives, and containers of plastic explosives. Wires, detonators, and sub-surface buoys trailed behind him. This was a "business trip."

As he neared the underwater mines he swam right up to the deadly metal balls. On their horns he taped blocks of TNT, and fastened lead wires. Some of them he disarmed, his fingers deft and sure as he unscrewed detonators. Any mistake would blow him to shreads, but he worked quickly and skillfully, tense with nervous anxiety.

On the underwater tank traps he taped high explosive charges or pressed blobs of plastic explosives. Fastened lead lines to quivering trip wires. Unreeled electric lead lines and trip lines. Strung them out into the deep water beyond the reef.

Busily he worked in the phosphorescent waters, connecting his lead lines to the marker buoy, floating just beyond the reef, under the surface. Then anchored the buoy, ready for the electric plunger detonator to be attached on the night before D-Day.

His underwater demolitions all set and ready, he turned towards the beach again. Intelligence HQ wanted him to find lanes of access off the beach and into the island. He cursed bitterly as he came up to the beach, and strode cautiously towards the tree line.

"What the hell do they want," he thought bitterly, "My blood?" But he went on.

Crossing the beach, he felt his skin crawl with fear. There were anti-personnel mines under the sand. not yet set off by bombardment. Any one of them might rip his naked legs into bloody tatters.

72

Up the beach, and into the trees. He moved like a shadow from tree to tree. Then an open space. He saw a narrow road. Marked it on his map. Saw a group of buildings back of a clear space. Barracks for the Japs! An attack down the road would run right into them. He noted the flat, open areas, good for flanking attacks.

Voices floated down the still air to him. The place was crawling with Japs. He had pushed his luck far enough. Silently he returned to the beach and started back towards his pickup line. It was near dawn when the rushing P.T. boat picked him up again.

"Another day, another dollar," he remarked wearily to one of his teammates as their boat roared out to sea.

D-Day was tomorrow morning. Off the shores of Eniwetok a vast fleet of American ships lay in the darkness. Thundering guns of warships made the night one roaring bedlam of sound and flashing, flaring lights of shellfire. Glowing projectiles streaked towards the island, to land in dancing, flickering eruptions. Deep in their dugouts and pillboxes the Japanese defenders cowered, as all hell raged roaring above them. Hour after hour the bombardment went on.

Aboard one troop transport, the *Middleton,* Dave Gould talked earnestly with the Marine platoon leaders whom he was to guide onto the beach.

"Get up the beach and through the narrow strip of woods fast," he urged. "Set your machine guns up damn fast. Then you can sweep the road and open space in front of the barracks—what's left of them. That's as far as I can lead you. Beyond that, it's up to you guys."

"Rodger dodger," answered a sergeant. "How come you didn't go into the barracks and map them too, frogman?"

"Your father's mustache!" said Gould. "What the hell do you guys want? Egg in your beer?"

In the landing craft. Gould crouched near the helmsman. He was not naked this time. Helmet, pistol, ammo belt, and full combat kit, ready for the assault. A frogman's work is not done until the beachhead is taken.

He pointed out landmarks and guided the helmsman as

73

the boat neared the reef. Overhead, screaming shells passed, bound for the shore, to keep the Japs down in their holes.

Just outside the reef the lead boat slowed almost to a stop. Gould stripped quickly. Picked up his plunger detonator, and dove into the green water. In nerve-tingling haste he searched for the marker buoy.

There it was! Treading water while sky and sea trembled under the bellowing cannonade, he fastened the lead wires to the electric detonator box. Pushed the plunger down, hard.

Before him, the whole beach seemed to erupt in one vast boiling wall of water, coral fragments, and pieces of flying metal. It was done, the way was open.

Eager hands hauled him from the water, back into the boat. There was no time for self-congratulation. Hastily he pulled on his combat clothing, over his wet skin. Buckled on his ammo belt and put his heavy steel helmet on his dripping hair. Checked the clip in his gun.

The first wave was coming in. He signalled with his hand. "Okay. All clear. Come on in!" His boat led the way, crunching onto the sand.

Silence seemed to shout suddenly at him. The bombardment had lifted off the beach. Then it began again, deeper inland, as his boat touched shore. Flights of planes screamed in, overhead, raking the battered area beyond the beach with bombs and guns. Only shattered stumps remained of the trees he had seen all along the shore.

From the pulverized trees and from half-buried pillboxes spouts of flames flickered out, and cracking sounds spat venemously. The Japs were still there, shooting at the invaders. Roar and counter-roar boomed along the shore. Sudden geysers of sand, dust and water flared and fell—mortar shells, bursting all up and down the beach.

*"Down ramp!"*

Men came leaping out of one boat after another as their ramps crashed open on the sand. His platoon of Marines, gathered in a group, looking expectantly towards him.

"That way—around the side of the pillbox!" He yelled

74

and pointed. His voice was drowned in the uproar, but his hand signal was plain. The men ran heavily up the beach, and dove to earth in the edge of shattered tree stumps.

*"Whap-p-p."*

His leg seemed to be pulled out from under him. Dull ache in his left leg, near the knee. He pulled himself half erect. He was down on the ground. Bright red patch near his left knee. Throbbing ache in his left thigh. He was hit.

For a moment his mind seemed blurred and hazy. Automatically he yanked his first aid packet from his belt. Wrapped the dressing around his leg, over the bloody trouser leg. Something stung and bit in his thigh muscle. A fragment of steel!

He couldn't stay on the beach. Faintly he heard a voice above the noise: "Goddamit! Gould, where the hell are you!"

Panting, he pulled himself erect, and stood up. No bones broken, anyhow.

"No bones broken, Dave." He was talking to himself. "You can navigate, boy! Get moving! Get off this damned beach!"

He hobbled heavily up the slope, and into the tangle of fallen trees. Inched forward to the edge facing the road and open space. Marines were crawling through it, moving forward.

In front of him two men were setting up a machine gun on the ground. He fell down beside them, just as one of them suddenly grunted and fell back, still and staring. The other man stared at him, and at his dead buddy, in dazed surprise.

Gould pulled himself into position behind the gun, and peered down its barrel. "Good field of fire," he thought, "right across the flat."

"Snap out of it, Mac!" he spat at the dazed assistant machine gunner. "Keep the belt feeding smooth. They'll be coming any second now."

Someone down the line yelled in a high, excited shriek: "Here they come!"

Across the open field a running line of men came

75

quickly towards them. Then more and more—hundreds of them. An officer led them, swinging his glittering samurai sword in circles over his head. They were screaming hysterically as they came.

"Banzai charge," Dave remarked, as if watching it at a movie. "Keep that feed belt smooth!"

He squeezed the trigger, and swung the machine gun from side to side in sweeping arcs. It stuttered into a long, tearing burst—*bub-bub-bub-bub-bub-bub-bub*—

Men were falling, out in the flat. Still others came on, endlessly, screaming like maniacs. The gun clattered on and on—*bap-bap-bap-bap-bap-bap*—

A red glow began to show as the barrel became overheated. It grew redder, as the gun hammered on and on—*bub-bub-bub-bub-bub*—

No time to change barrels now. The barrel seemed to quiver and squirm as he sighted along it. It could not last much longer.

Then they were gone! Disappeared, as though they had evaporated. The field was full of twisted, sprawled bodies. Dully, Gould wondered how many his gun had killed. He felt sick and faint. Nausea welled up in his chest. His leg suddenly hurt like hell. It was getting dark. Queer, getting dark so early in the morning! Whirling, roaring noise in his head. He fell forward. Dark—— dim——dark.

Dave Gould woke up aboard the *Middleton,* two days later. He had been carried back by corpsmen. His leg was sore and a bit stiff, but not crippled. Aside from loss of blood, shock, and exhaustion, he was intact. "Able to fight another day!" the medic told him sardonically.

And so indeed it was to be. Dave Gould was to go in again and again with the U.D.T.—at Kwajalein, Palau, Leyte, and other bitter beaches.

Quietly, without glamor or glory, he was to do, again and again, the hardest, most dangerous job that any man can do—the job of the *combat frogman.*

Glory didn't interest this quiet, smiling young man from the big city. He was to return to New York a Chief

Petty Officer, eager to return to the work of production rather than destruction.

Dave Gould lives in a quiet apartment on Riverside Drive now, high above New York's Hudson River. Like so many Americans, he is utterly unimpressed with his own deeds. "Look," he says "the war was a dirty job that had to be done. So we did it. I was suited for frogman combat, so that's what they put me in. That's all."

He works quietly, hard, and efficiently for American Car and Foundry Company now, as a Fabrication Superintendent. Doesn't expect ever to get rich, but takes good care of his wife and young daughter. Goes to Campbell Inn, in the mountains at Roscoe, New York, for summer vacations. Teaches his daughter Karen, and the other kids there, how to swim, in the cool, spotless swimming pool.

Dave can't swim underwater much, nowadays. One eardrum was punctured by an underwater mine burst in the Philippines, in his last battle.

Life can be wryly ironic, though, even in times of peace, for the "quiet man" kind of fellow like Dave Gould. Last spring he was strolling with Frances, his wife, along a walk in Riverside Park, one evening. Six young juvenile delinquents stalked them, as easy game for a quick mugging and robbery. Dave is not a big man, and doesn't look or act tough.

But when the six young hoodlums surrounded them, Dave Gould remembered the deadly hand-to-hand lessons of his war days. Within a minute three of the young punks were lying unconscious on the ground, one was cowering in Dave's grip, and the others were running in terror.

That is Dave Gould, an average looking fellow, now in his early forties. Quiet, hard-working, family man, with no liking for violence.

Dave Gould—like so many other peaceful Americans. Salt-of-the-earth men, to whom duty, honor and courage are "taken for granted" things.

Quiet men, who make America great.

# THEY COULDN'T BE LICKED

### By Victor R. Donaghue

"Squirrel-headed generals." That, said the newspapers in mid-1956, is what former President Harry Truman called the planners of the Salerno invasion—Operation *Avalanche*.

What the G.I.'s and British Tommys called them in 1943 was a lot more pungent. The wisdom or folly of that first major invasion of Europe will be argued for years to come. It was the nearest the Allies came to utter defeat and disaster.

Yet, one fact remains sure. Dangerous and doubtful as it was, the Salerno landing *did* win out. Generals who *win* can't be as stupid as armchair critics may say.

Ask the veterans of the 36th Infantry Division, the 45th Infantry Division, the Rangers, and the 82nd Airborne Division, about bloody Salerno. Ask the men of the cruiser *U.S.S. Savannah*. Ask the tough Limeys of the British 46th and 56th Divisions and Commando. Then watch the air turn blue as they talk about "that goddam filthy, Salerno beachhead."

On September 3rd, 1943, right after Sicily was secured, General Montgomery slipped two British divisions across the Strait of Messina, onto the toe of the Italian boot. His slow drive up the mountainous peninsula easily could be stopped by the Germans—unless another invasion was made farther north.

The bay of Salerno was the logical place, just at the extreme limit of Allied fighter-plane range. There the major supply port of Naples could be seized, and the airfields at Foggia. The only trouble was that this logic was as obvious to the Germans as it was to the Yanks and English.

The Italian fascists had surrendered, and the Germans

78

were hurriedly reinforcing the threatened area. They had eighteen veteran divisions, led by the wily Field Marshal Kesserling, to throw against four Allied divisions. From the frowning heights all around the 30-mile-wide, semi-circular Salerno Bay, big German guns commanded the entire invasion area.

Eisenhower, the Supreme Commander, decided to give command of the invading Fifth Army to General Mark Clark. This was Clark's first battle command. The British X Corps' divisions would land on the north, with their Commandos and American Rangers. The American VI Corps would land the 36th Division first, in the south, and then the 45th Division.

On September 8th some 450 ships, commanded by Vice-Admiral Henry K. Hewitt, U.S.N., moved into the beautiful Tyrrhenian Sea and approached the shores of Salerno Bay. On his flagship *Ancon* Clark watched the scurrying landing craft head for the wide-curving beaches.

Some of the fanciful dreams of the Allies soon were to be blown sky high. They had theorized that the Germans would pull back to northern Italy, if attacked in force. Instead, at Salerno and every step of the way, the Germans showed them that every inch of Italy would be savagely contested. The hard, bitter fighting was to begin at Salerno.

Air experts had said confidently that air superiority would cut German supply lines and force the enemy to retreat. Allied bombers of Air Marshal Tedder's Anglo-American forces plastered enemy communications for weeks, then months, and finally years—in vain.

Later, Clark said that the air power theory "was a complete flop. The Germans kept right on increasing their strength in Italy until the very end and were able to battle us for every foot of Italian soil."

In the end it was to be the personal fighting abilities of the plain GI and Tommy that decided the outcome. Be the high command's plans good, bad, or indifferent, one factor remained certain. Against the tough, experienced German fighting men, came stubbornly determined Yanks and Limey fighting men, to win out in brutal,

79

face-to-face combat. *They* were the ultimate victors, not the military "geniuses," theorists, or commanders.

It was typical at Salerno. When the landing craft neared the heavily defended beaches, German loudspeakers bellowed triumphantly out at them: "We've got you covered. Come ashore and surrender!" Flares shot into the dark pre-dawn sky, to light up the ominous beaches. German guns sited on the shore, opened up with a terrific roar.

The Americans and British came in, but not to surrender. They came in fighting and shooting, driving hard up the beaches, to grapple with their enemy. German planes, artillery, and machine guns raked the wide-open beaches. Landing craft lurched, shook, and sank under a storm of explosives and screaming rockets and shells. But more came on, undaunted. Men whose boats had been shot out from under them swam and waded ashore and, gasping in exhaustion, pushed stubbornly up the shore.

The record of individual bravery and gallantry is far too long to repeat. Just for example, take Private Jim Logan. From behind a wall a German machine gun raked the spot where he crouched. Three Germans, firing rifles as they came on, rushed out to finish him off. With rapid fire sharpshooting he nailed all of them—one, two, three. Then he picked off the machine gunners. And then, using the German gun, he blasted several other Kraut gunners as they fled from this one-man terror.

Or take Private Jim C. Jones. He found about fifty stragglers from decimated landing boat groups lying flat on the beach under a storm of fire. He took command, led them up the beach, through a howling gale of flying steel. Then he led them, in dash after dash, to silence one machine gun post after another.

Or Sergeant Manuel Gonzales, pinned down by an 88 mm. gun firing pointblank, with Kraut riflemen all around. He crawled on his belly through the stabbing, searching fire, while potato-masher grenades burst all around him. Then, close to the looming "88," he pitched grenades into the emplacement, to kill the entire gun crew.

Or take such heroic little units as the Rangers up north near Maiori, led by Lt. Col. Bill Darby. Their orders were to seize and hold high ground on the left flank of the invasion area, as an anchor for the landings. They seized a commanding hilltop, and held it through day after day of furious counterattacks.

By nightfall the town of Salerno was taken. In their first battle, the men of the 36th Division had driven five miles ahead. The 45th Division had come ashore and had pushed miles inland too. That night it was to meet swarming German tanks and infantry head on, forcing its spearheads to withdraw. The vastly larger German forces were gathering, to try to drive the invaders into the sea. On the surrounding heights the Germans could look down the throats of the invasion force.

Five Panzer-troop divisions stabbed at the beachhead from every direction, while hordes of Nazi infantry pressed down from the hills all around. Salerno was pure misery.

By September 12th the whole perimeter of the beachhead was one roaring wall of fire and blazing battle. Kesserling had announced that he would drive the invaders into the sea. German bombers and attack planes roared over the area almost unopposed, despite the Allies' theoretical air superiority. Panzer spearheads drove into the middle of the beleaguered invasion force, trying to split it in half. German radio propaganda chortled the prediction that the whole operation was a ridiculous mistake, soon to be utterly smashed and "liquidated."

GIs and Tommys dug in and held on, while roaring waves of attack smashed at them. Their pitifully outnumbered units clawed desperately at whole divisions that came clanking and screaming at them in seemingly endless waves.

Hastily, General Clark called back to the rear, back in Sicily, for reinforcements. Only an airdrop by the 82nd Airborne could possibly arrive in time to help at all.

The final catastrophe seemed to be a breakthrough at Persano. An enemy tank-led spearhead was pushing right into the rear areas, hardly two miles from the shore. The Americans had absolutely no reserve units with which to stop it. The 36th Division staggered back under re-

81

peated, massive assaults. Had Kesserling fully realized his opportunity, and rushed more troops in, the Germans probably would have annihilated the invaders. They had over 600 tanks at Salerno.

In the depth of this gloomy moment Clark spotted a critical hill right in the path of the breakthrough. This was soon to be known as *Piccolo Peak,* for a bitter-humor reason.

The only men not yet engaged in battle were those of a regimental band and some clerks, mechanics and truck drivers. The musicians were issued weapons and placed on *Piccolo Peak.* The clerks, mechanics and truck drivers, plus six 37 mm. guns and crews borrowed from the 45th Division's 189th and 158th Field Artillery Battalions, dug in nearby.

This almost laughable mixture of GIs opened up on the approaching German tanks. Piccolo players blew a dance of death at the Huns, and clerks filed bullets and shells in their vehicles, while mechanics and truck drivers hurled assorted hardware at them.

After several baffled and frightened thrusts, the Germans wavered, and then turned back, followed by blazing fire from the now enthusiastic amateur killers. The next morning planes of the 82nd's 504th Parachute Regiment came droning over, dropping their hell-for-leather paratroopers right into the lines.

The Germans were not yet licked. Their commanders drove them forward again and again, in constant attacks. But somehow the spirit seemed to have gone out of the Huns. They had struck with everything they had, only to be beaten back by a ragged, bobtailed bunch of Yank amateurs. Then, on top of that, the terrible, laughing paratroopers of the 82nd—some of the toughest killers in history—had leaped on them from the sky.

It was too much. How could you defeat men who simply would not quit! Men who attacked when they should have surrendered! The grim, stubborn, tooth-and-claw resistance of the outnumbered Yanks took the heart out of the Germans.

To cap the climax for the Germans, next day, on September 14th, came the long-heralded Allied air assault.

American and British planes in swarming squadrons blasted communication lines and supply dumps, while strafing planes ripped and tore, to and fro, over the German positions. The big guns of the warships in the bay, directed from the beachhead, hurled salvos of 15- and 16-inch shells onto the disheartened Krauts. The effects of this combined bombardment were devastating. For the first time at Salerno the German superiority in men and material was overmatched by a greater weight of flying metal.

As a follow-up Clark ordered the 509th Parachute Regiment of the 82nd Airborne to drop near Avellino that night. This was the first paratroop drop behind enemy lines, and took heavy losses. Clark was criticized for such a hazardous decision. Very few paratroopers could break through back to the lines. But they hid in the hills, raising general hell with the German rear areas, and within two months 80 percent of them safely returned to the American lines.

Soon after, when Eisenhower came to visit the Salerno front, Clark recommended the relief of General Dawley from command of VI Corps. This action was intended to restore the self-confidence of the battered 36th and 45th Divisions. They had fought magnificently, but had suffered from the uneven combat. Major General John Lucas was given command by Eisenhower.

In the week of constant savage fighting the casualty lists had grown to serious proportions. Actually the British sector had suffered heavier attacks than the Americans. British X Corps had lost 531 men killed, 1915 wounded and 1561 missing. American VI Corps, with only half as many men as the British had there, had lost 225 men killed, 853 wounded, and 589 missing. Many of the men listed as missing in the confused melees later turned up safe and sound as units straightened themselves out.

Reconnaisance units reported that the Germans were withdrawing. The bloody fighting had cost them dearly, many times heavier than the Allies. Almost every one of their divisions had been terribly mauled—the 16th Panzer Division, 15th Panzer Grenadier Division, Herman

83

Goering Armored Division, 26th Panzer Grenadier Division, 3rd Panzer Grenadier Division, and many attached regiments, battalions, and special units.

So began the endless, heartbreaking drive north up the rough Italian peninsula. It was to be a long, costly campaign, where every advantage of ground favored the Germans. But its ends could be foretold surely.

Salerno was the keynote. There the basic test of fighting men against fighting men had been made, once and for all. The result of that test had been plain, in dead and maimed men, blood, sweat and pain.

There it had been made clear that the GI and the Tommy were better fighting men than the much vaunted "Herrenvolk." The American and Briton were more stubborn, more aggressive, tougher, and wilier than the German.

Man for man the German was whipped at Salerno—and he knew it. Whether or not the landing there was a wise command decision or not, that vital fact was proved. And that was more important than any command decision.

It foretold what was to be the outcome of the greatest war in history in letters of fire.

# THE BLOODIEST RAID OF THE WAR

## By George Hanks

ODDLY ENOUGH, it wasn't the first raid on Ploesti. Twelve B-24's based in Egypt had penetrated the Axis air defenses around the oil fields on June 12, 1942. They'd dumped their bomb loads without too much trouble.

"Proof that a large-scale raid can succeed," Whitehall is said to have declared.

But the Germans had been given more than a year since then to strengthen their defenses around Ploesti. Furthermore, because of the way the war was going, the Ploesti oil fields and refineries were far more important to the Nazis than they had been in 1942.

"This'll be rougher than a cob," said Lt. Bob Jennings, our plane commander, shaking his head, after our first briefing on July 29, 1943. "I don't like it—not one bit."

We were based on Bengasi in Libya. The operations order for the attack on Ploesti called for every available B-24 Liberator on the base to be used against the target. The sweep was to take place on August 1st.

I was belly gunner on the "Fagged-Out Floozie," a Lib that had seen its share of action in North Africa. The old gooney bird was almost ready for the scrap heap—and now they wanted us to shove it across the Mediterranean and deep into enemy territory!

"Do they expect any of us to get back?" I asked grimly.

"Sure!" Jennings growled. "Everybody's bubbling with optimism. They're saying it's going to be a milk run!"

"None of those people flying the raid, I suppose?"

"Of course not! That's why they're so optimistic!"

The Ploesti refineries were deep inside Roumania, north of Bucharest, the capital. It was a long, long flight

85

from Libya to Roumania. Round-trip, the hop meant almost 3000 miles of steady flying—if we took a straight, air-line course.

"Which, of course, we won't be allowed to do," groaned Charlie Backer, our needle-nosed navigator. "They'll make us criss-cross half the hemisphere to get where we're going."

There were 180 B-24's lined up before dawn on August 1, 1943. Every one of the slab-sided, four-engined Libs were gassed to the limit and loaded with all the bombs and machine gun ammo they could carry.

Lieutenant Jennings checked us as we climbed aboard the Fagged-Out Floozie. We were clumsy and awkward in our flying suits, with out pockets stuffed with candy, sandwiches, and fruit.

"Okay," he muttered. "Climb in—and wait."

A warm wind blew across the Bengasi airfield. It brought sand that scratched against the metal fuselages and wing surfaces of the 24's.

I crammed myself down into the belly turret and made a final inspection. Everything looked in order. There would be nothing more I could do until we were up and rendezvousing, and I ground off a burst or two to make sure the 50's were working.

At long last—after a wait that seemed days but was only a few minutes—the Libs began cranking up. One ship—then four—then eight—then the whole field was filled with the thunder of engines.

Then it was our turn. Our big mills caught one by one.

The big ships lumbered into take-off position. They waited for the go-ahead from the control tower, and then waddled into the wind until they were airborne. We were about the fiftieth to go. When Jennings got the signal, we were off to the Ploesti races. But there were no bets on this course.

By the time we rendezvoused, there were only 177 Liberators in the flight. Two had crashed on takeoff, one aborted. It wasn't a bad showing. The beatup old Libs had held up fairly well.

86

We banked and headed over the Mediterranean. We cleared our guns, firing them down into the water. I climbed out of the belly turret and lay down on the floor. We were a long way from any possible enemy interception. There would be plenty of time to squeeze myself into the tiny turret later.

The hours passed slowly. Ben Cohen, the starboard waist gunner, dug out some meat sandwiches he'd scrounged from the squadron mess and shared them with me. The meat was tough and we chewed like hell.

"Nothing's too good for our boys, eh?" Ben yelled sourly. "Those bastards back home must be killing rhinoceroses and selling the meat as beef."

The weather was clear and the sun bright when we finally got over Roumania. We'd run into light flak and fighter opposition here and there, but we'd gotten through the ack-ack and driven off the enemy ships without loss or damage.

We by-passed Bucharest, then started to let down! We were about to commit suicide.

The Ploesti raid had been planned as a low-level bombing sweep! The huge, four-engined bombers were to come in at rooftop level—as if they were tactical aircraft strafing enemy troops!

"They'll never expect it at that altitude," the planners back at Bengasi had promised. "They'll be all shaken up . . ."

I eased myself into my turret. Flak was coming up—plenty of it. It was black and deadly. The Lib bounced and rocked from the concussions. Ploesti was still ten or fifteen minutes away and already flights of FW 190's were coming up from all sides. We were pretty well back and in the center of the formation. They weren't into us—yet . . .

It started. The intercom got hot.

"Bandit, three o'clock . . . Bandits, two at nine o'clock . . ."

Cohen was firing from his starboard station. The new kid in the tail cut loose. I caught a flash of Focke-Wulfe

87

and swung the turret. The Kraut was boring in from ahead and below. I led him, and triggered my guns.

The tracers smoked out, and the FW veered off without attacking. I brought up the barrels and traversed. For the moment, the sky was clear of fighters, but one Lib was going down, trailing smoke. The flak started again.

We were down low—so low that it was almost senseless for me to sit in the belly turret. Nothing could come up from under us. I felt as though I could reach out and grab handfuls of leaves from the tops of the trees over which we were skimming.

In the next instant, the whole carefully planned mission began to be blown to pieces. It was only the beginning of the end—for the mass-murder took time—endless time the way we lived through it, those of us who did live through it.

The lead ships started to go down almost immediately. The Nazis and their Roumanian stooges weren't shaken up. They were ready and expecting us. They'd tracked us all the way from Libya. They had us taped and zeroed.

Their ack-ack was shooting short-fused. The 88 gunners were cutting their fuses to a hair past muzzle-burst point. Their quad 40's and 20's threw up solid curtains and sheets of blasting high explosive.

"It's a trap—it's a goddam trap!"

The words came over my earphones. I don't know who said them. I do know that the man who yelled them sobbed and groaned. I was in a capsule, cut off from the rest of the plane. I was down in the ball turret, hanging from the belly like some fragile, plexiglass scrotum dangling from a bird flying directly into the hunters' guns!

There were railroad tracks and sidings below me. The Fagged-Out Floozie held on its course and flashed over the rail yards. Here and there, a great sheet of flame marked the spot where a Lib had crashed or flown into the ground.

The German fighter pilots were smarter than they'd been given credit for being. They didn't try to come up from beneath or hit us from above. They knew we were holding our bomb-run course. They stayed at the side and swept in to rake the formation.

"Bandits . . . bandits . . . there must be hundreds of them . . . !"

The intercom never stopped scratching and jabbering. We were getting everything. But the real hell, the terrible slaughter of Ploesti was seconds away.

"Pull up! For God's sake, start hauling up!"

The pilots were near panic. Suddenly, the sky was filled with weapons no one had dreamed existed at Ploesti. We were flying straight into a forest!

I saw the forest—dozens and scores of deadly barrage balloons shooting up from free-wheeling winches on the ground. My turret was facing forward. I'd just sprayed a burst at an FW and had squared off with the fuselage. I saw the balloons and the cables—and I saw the B-24's hit them, shear off wings—and plunge earthward.

"Good God!" It was Jennings' voice. "They've got us!"

The ship tipped as he hauled back on the wheel. The nose went up. Then we were clawing and fighting for altitude. We had to get above the balloons. They were everywhere. The enemy was running them up—and fast.

"All gunners: shoot down the damn things to give the guys behind us a chance . . ."

I trained my guns. I saw one, and opened fire. It exploded. There were balloons on all sides. I let go at another. It, too, exploded. Below, a burning B-24 slammed into the ground. A second spun in.

Suddenly, our Lib jounced and practically stood up on its port wing. We'd been hit. There was a gaping hole in the starboard wing. It was big enough to let a man slide through easily. Bits of metal shredded from the hole and were carried back by the slipstream.

"Okay—? Everyone okay?"

We reported in. No one was hurt. Then we were on our final leg. Jennings turned the ship over to Pratt, the bombardier. The refineries were below.

"Bomb bay doors open . . ."

There were fires and secondary explosions below. The ship rose suddenly, as if pushed up by a giant hand.

"Bombs away!"

The Lib went up like an elevator when the bombs dropped from the racks because of the suddenly lessened weight. I saw the salvoed bombs fall. They'd all gone—there was nothing left in the bay.

"Bomb bay doors closed. Let's get the hell out of here . . . !"

Jennings banked the Lib. I could now see the Ploesti refineries spread out behind us. There were clouds of smoke and fires, but far less of both than I figured I'd be seeing. I watched the scene below for a few seconds—and then the grim, dangerous business of fighting our way through the Nazi defenses began again.

"Jesus! They've got Mac!"

Jack MacDowell was the pilot of the bomber on our right. The ship took a direct hit—probably from an 88. It disintegrated in mid-air. I saw the chunks and pieces hurtle earthward. I looked for chutes— There were none.

"Bandits—bandits at one o'clock high . . ."

"Bandits at three o'clock . . ."

I had my hands full. A Focke-Wulfe bored in. Its wing guns were winking. I got him sighted in and tripped the solenoid. My streams of tracers jabbed out at him—wide. I adjusted a fraction and the slugs ate into his wing stubs. The FW appeared to stop in midair. Then it flipped over and went down.

There was a roaring explosion above me. The Lib shivered and shook. We'd taken another hit—this time in the waist. The ship rocked and slewed, and Jennings fought to get it back under control.

"I—I think Cohen's dead!"

Backer came out of his navigator's station to check. He found Cohen sprawled over his waist gun, his head practically torn off. The other waist gun was knocked out —the gunner bleeding badly.

"We can still fly. Shall we try and make it—or do you guys want to bail?" Jennings asked us to make the decision. We did.

"Try and take her in, Bob . . ."

We got past the Ploesti hot-spot and closed up our

90

formations. There were gaps—plenty of them. We'd taken a hell of a beating. Of the 177 B-24's that had started the mission, 54 were shot down!

Jennings nursed the battered Floozie back to Bengasi after we had jettisoned everything that was loose inside the ship. One engine was acting up—and finally went out. Another coughed and sputtered and threatened to quit at any minute.

We shot the customary red flare showing we had wounded aboard when we came in on the base leg of our approach to the field at Bengasi.

"Better take your turn," came the grimly agonized voice of the control tower operator. "There's hardly a ship that doesn't . . ."

We'd been luckier than most of the others. We had only one dead man aboard—Ben Cohen. The other waist gunner was badly hurt, but would live. Lieutenant Pratt, the bombardier, was wounded, too, but it wasn't serious.

More than 600 officers and men were lost on the Ploesti raid—a bloody blunder.

The Ploesti refineries?

So well had the installations been defended that we inflicted only light damage on the refineries!

Production was "interrupted" for a week or two. But the Nazi engineers had the refineries operating again before August 15th!

It wasn't until 1944 that the refineries were knocked out. Then, we had long-range fighter planes to give us cover and we were flying from Italian bases.

A few weeks after the ill-fated raid, sometime during September or October, 1943, our crew was listening to a radio broadcast over BBC. The English announcer was discussing the theory that the Nazis could be best defeated by attacking them through the Balkans.

"The Germans are most vulnerable in the 'soft underbelly of Europe,' " the announcer said.

We looked at each other. Nobody said anything. Then Jennings got up and walked over to the radio. It was the

91

only set in the squadron that worked. He drew back his foot and kicked it across the room.

None of us objected. We all understood how he felt. We felt the same way . . .

# I WAS A GUARD ON THE
# BATAAN DEATH MARCH

### By Yasua Kata

ON APRIL 10TH, 1942, I was an interpreter in the Imperial Japanese Army working out of Olongapo Base on Subic Bay. I was on Bataan for special duty at the request of the *Kempetai,* or military police. American prisoners were being sent from southern Bataan up to San Fernando Pamanga. I was with a group who would meet them at the midpoint of the sixty-mile journey and escort them to the rail head. There, others would load the prisoners on trains and ship them to Capas in Tarlac Province. From there, they would be walked to their destination, Camp O'Donnell. The officer to take charge of our area would be a Captain Umara. I knew about the Captain from talk around the base. He was a member of *Kokuryu Kai,* the Black Dragon Society. He was part of the military clique that hacked up several conservatives at home. To date, he hadn't met an armed enemy.

Several men waited for the Captain with me. They were members of the crack Fifth Division Tokyo Guards. They started out as a platoon but had run into a mine on the way up. There were now three. One was a youngster so new he carried a 7.7 mm. rifle, which would later see service as our Model 99, and which none of the rest of us had seen until that moment. The other two were battle-wise soldiers. One they called "Ox" looked big, mean, and dumb, and carried several healed scars on his face and neck. The second, I barely saw because he kept hidden in the deep coogan grass throughout our wait, refusing to offer a sniper a target for a minute. These men were to be the Captain's personal guards.

A cyclist appeared about then, and the youngster hurried over to join the crowd that formed around him. He stopped long enough for a drink of water and to stretch himself and was on his way. The boy ran back to us bringing news.

"The march has started. They started to move yesterday. They should be on us at any time." His eyes were wide. "The prisoners come in groups of a thousand each." He looked around at our relatively small number.

"Don't worry, I will protect you," the Ox grinned, and he stroked the boy's cheek. The youngster shook the hand off. The man in the grass crawled out and joined us.

"I don't like it either," he said, "we may be too few to control a thousand men."

"They would have nowhere to go if they did escape," I suggested. He shook his head.

"They might decide they are better off dead and try to take us along with them."

"The cyclist said they were sick and weak and many couldn't even walk," the boy offered hopefully.

"They once told us they couldn't fight in jungles also," the older man said grimly. The Ox started to sneer and the smaller man turned on him like a cat. The bigger man stopped grinning and backed off sullenly. The little man was cautious, but evidently very tough.

"Kata," I introduced myself.

"Tamura," he returned, surveying the area. "I would feel easier with a couple of heavy Hotchkiss guns covering those points." He gestured. "Let's hope the captain isn't a complete idiot."

"He's here, we'll soon see," I said, watching a captured jeep roll into the clearing. An officer was standing up even while it was in motion. Now, as it stopped, he was yelling orders in a harsh, rasping voice. Captain Umara was with us.

The captain was tall and very thin. He wore a sword and a heavy pistol. He informed us that several columns were moving up behind us as re-enforcements. However, he pointed out that the few men we had would be enough to control the prisoners because men who surrendered in battle were cowards, and by simply being Japanese we were superior.

Tamura blew his nose loudly. The captain looked at him and showed his annoyance. Tamura returned a gaze of such innocence that it was obvious he had made the noise deliberately.

The captain went on to outline his plan for handling the Americans. It was sound and simple. They wouldn't try anything during the change of men because they faced double the number of guards. The most they might hope for at that time would be a breather. Instead, we would jump them quickly and force them into quicker paces, which we could stand as we were rested. By the time we let the pace fall off they would be too tired to start anything.

"Any breech of discipline," the captain ordered, "is punishable by death. In such cases you will use your bayonets when possible so you will have rifles ready at all times."

"What if they cannot continue to keep the pace?" someone asked.

"That is a breech of discipline," he said, pleasantly. It was obvious we couldn't leave the fallen men free behind us, nor spare our own men from guard duty to cover them. Execution was the only answer, but it wasn't the reason the captain gave.

"We will not disturb ourselves over those who will fall," he said. "They cannot expect the rules of Bushido to apply to creatures who hold themselves so low as not to fight to the death." At that point, the captain looked very noble.

Tamura blew his nose loudly again. Before the captain could take offense, a sound drew our attention elsewhere. There was an increasing rumble of sound in which yells, shots, and screams intermingled with the crashing through brush of many men. The prisoners were arriving.

The strongest prisoners came in first. They were emaciated, starved, and tattered but they were moving at a fair pace. Behind them, the line slowed in direct proportion to the weakness and injuries among the prisoners

95

there. The guards were policing the lines, kicking and prodding them along. One of them brought up an American officer to request an audience with the officer in charge. Captain Umara motioned him over to us. The man saluted our captain, who ignored him.

"Captain," he said, "my men have been without water for nearly two days. We must have water." His own tongue was badly swollen and consequently his speech was hard to understand. The captain indicated that he should repeat his request.

"We must have water," the officer said.

"Tell him his army should have thought about that when they sent men into battle and been prepared for it." I quickly translated the captain's answer.

"The Japs took our canteens," the prisoner said indignantly.

"It is necessary we have all aluminum metal for the war effort," the Captain advised him. And dismissed him with a wave of his hand. The guard who had brought him shoved him back into the moving crowd. By that time, our men were in position. The captain screamed the order to start marching and took off as an example at a double-quick step. A groan went up from the prisoners but they did their best to follow. We went at that pace for perhaps thirty yards until the captain slowed down to a walk and finally stopped altogether to watch the prisoners pass by.

One of our men came up. He saluted and waited for the captain's permission to speak.

"Some of the prisoners demand to stop by the road," he said when Umara nodded to him, "for biological reasons."

"No stopping, it will slow us down," the Captain said. The soldier shuffled uneasily, "They have dysentery."

"No stopping," the Captain repeated and he shoved the man with his palm. He looked up and down the moving column. Men were squatting along the road every few feet. The Captain started for them with a scream of rage. He interrupted a prisoner who had just reached the roadside.

96

"No stopping," he yelled at him. I translated. The man looked at me wide-eyed.

"I'm dying of these cramps, what can I do?" he asked me.

"The captain orders you not to stop." He looked over at Yumara. "Ask the brass what the hell he thinks a man is made of!" the prisoner said in disgust. The captain didn't bother calling for a translation. He kicked the stricken man in the belly. He folded quietly and lay there.

Two prisoners stepped out of the column and braced the fallen man under the armpits and dragged him with them. They knew his fate if left there.

While we stood there, a tall man worked his way to the side of the road. His face was stark white and he clutched his belly. He made clear gestures to the guard as to his intent. The guard looked briefly over at the captain and blocked the man's path. The pause was more than the prisoner could take. He stained himself with slime and blood then stood shocked at his lack of ability to control himself. Suddenly, he started to weep. The captain approached him brandishing his sword. The man looked like an animal in shock, evidently realizing the threat, but was more concerned with the pain of the blow. He flinched under the expected blow. That pleased the captain. He stopped in front of the man.

"Stopping is not permitted," he said. The prisoner didn't understand him but he had reached the end of his personal rope. He looked at the captain.

"Get the hell out of my way, ape," he said and pushed past him toward the brush. He stopped and loosened his filthy clothes. The captain looked around briefly to be certain he was thoroughly covered. The Ox and the boy flanked him with arms at ready. The captain walked up behind the tall man and swung the flat of his two-handed sword against the back of the man's head. It knocked him flat. Before he could recover himself the Ox was on him smashing his rifle butt down against his kidneys. He dropped flat and moved around slowly. The Ox stood over him with his bayonet poised for a thrust.

"Stopping is not allowed!" the captain screamed at the fallen man. "Make him move." And he strode off. I started to follow him and from the corner of my eye saw the beaten American trying to pull himself up on his arms. Even as I turned I caught the sickened look on the boy's face. Then I saw the Ox push the man flat with his foot and drive the bayonet into his back.

When I caught up with the captain, he already had two more culprits lined up. One was on his knees, the second stood near him holding his hand as a child holds a battered but precious toy. They turned to me in relief when they realized I spoke their language. I explained the captain's orders.

"We're sick," the one standing explained, "we can't help it. You'll wind up having to kill every man in camp, we all have the trots." I relayed what he said to the captain. He had to admit there was some truth in what the man said.

"It is not allowed, so they must be punished," he reasoned. "Tell them they must eat their own dirt." I told them what he wanted. They looked at each other in dumb horror and neither moved. The captain assumed that they didn't understand his command and made gestures to clarify his order. The one on his knees began to retch. The standing one looked at him in disbelief, then reached for the captain in speechless fury. The Ox shot him through the body. He crumpled on top of his friend, crushing him to the ground. The other worked himself from under him in tears to find the Ox's rifle barrel pressed to his head. He looked around at us realizing that this was his last chance at life. His fingers dropped into the bloody slime, then slowly started toward his dark, tortured, tear-stained face.

"*Yedo*, pure spirit of *Yedo*," a voice said behind me. Tamura had come up behind us as the incident had closed. *Yedo* is the old name for Tokyo and in Japan it is used as the incarnation of chivalry. I returned his nod.

"They want you up ahead," he said. I moved forward with him. One of our men was holding several prisoners at bay with his rifle. He said they were breaking off leaves to suck on as they moved along. It was their only form of moisture. The guard wanted to know if it was allowed.

"The leaves don't belong to you," I told him sharply. "Let them eat the trees themselves, as long as they keep moving."

"Who gave you permission to give orders?" Captain Umara asked.

"I gave it in your name," I snapped without turning, "before this idiot and a few others let themselves be drawn in among the prisoners to dig out a few leaves." He was willing to concede a point where his own safety was concerned. He said nothing and moved off. Tamura looked after him. There was an open sneer on his face, and I was certain that the captain saw it.

The trail began to tighten at this point. The heavy growth pushed down against the path in a thick, almost impenetrable tangle. The guards and prisoners were thrown together too closely for my liking. I said as much to Tamura.

"I don't like this place, either," he agreed. "If there are guerrillas in the area, they will hit us here." He moved up ahead and approached the captain. I noticed the captain was being covered by the boy alone and looked around for the Ox. I located him off the road a bit, beating a young Filipino across the face with a belt wrapped around his fist.

"What do you think you are doing?" I asked him. He turned cold eyes on me.

"What does *Baboui* mean?" he demanded in a rage. I knew if I told him it meant pig he would kill the youngster and I had a fair idea why the Ox had hauled the boy off the road and why the boy had cursed him.

"It's like their *Sus Maria,* a sort of prayer," I told him easily. "You better get back to the captain before he finds you missing." I took the boy out of his grasp and shoved him among the moving prisoners.

The captain was standing and drinking water. He told us he had sent Tamura up ahead to scout the area and we would proceed with caution even though he knew the area was secure. He arranged himself with the Ox behind him so that no sniper could take him without hitting the Ox first, and the boy on his outer flank for the same reason. I was given the honor of leading the way in case there was a grenade set waiting.

We moved on for perhaps a half a mile and suddenly found ourselves in a large clearing. Tamura waited, pressed against the roots of a giant tree, mostly hidden as usual. He pointed up ahead without a word.

There was a small flap tent rigged as a sun shade under which several of the brass lounged, watching for the approach of the prisoners. They were flanked on the sides by heavy Hotchkiss 7.7 mm. machine guns of the new 01 type.

Our captain wasted no time running over to his superiors, he evidently assumed if they were there, no harm threatened. He was probably right. They saluted him casually and sent him on his way. They sat there so that the parched prisoners could watch them drink. From time to time, when they noticed a particularly parched American, one of them would pour some liquid on the ground and they would all laugh. One of the prisoners worked his way up beside me as we moved on.

"You are the one who speaks English, aren't you?" he asked. I nodded that I did. "Is that no way of getting some water, any kind of water?" he asked, then quickly added, "for the sicker men I mean." I shook my head.

"We only have what is in our canteens, there is no other," I told him.

"Where can we get water, finally?" he asked, and I realized the thought of water possessed him to a point where even discussing it was a relief. I turned and asked Tamura. He answered without taking his eyes from the tree tops he was searching. "At O'Donnell probably, the Bamban River is only three miles from it."

I told this to the man who spoke to me.

"That must be twenty or thirty miles from here," he said desperately, "none of us will make it."

I shrugged.

"Isn't there anything along here that we can use, a creek, a well, a spring, anything?"

I told him I didn't know the area. We walked further and he turned again.

100

"Is the Bamban water drinkable?" I relayed the question to Tamura who by now was moving along like a hunting cat. He answered offhand.

"It isn't *Sakurayu*," his reference was to a drink which is a delicacy among our people. It is made of hot water with salt and cherry blossoms added.

"It's foul," I advised the prisoner. He shook his head gravely.

"There probably isn't one water-purifying pill among the lot of us. The dysentery will kill half the camp," he said.

I moved away from him. As I did so, I could feel a dozen pair of eyes glued to my water bottle. They must have been praying that the talk would lead to a taste of water for one of them.

There was more commotion ahead. I ran forward. The captain and his guards reached there the same time as I did. Several of the prisoners had come upon a small puddle by the side of the road. The radiator of an auto or something similar had broken and the discolored water had not soaked completely into the ground. Several men had thrown themselves on it and were licking at it wildly.

"It is not allowed!" the captain screamed. "It is a breach of discipline." He had the guards shoot them where they lay. He was stamping around pointing out his handiwork to the passing prisoners when Tamura doubled back to him. There was something happening up ahead. It could be a trap. The captain immediately covered himself with his arrangement of men as shields and gave Tamura permission to move ahead of us. I walked a few feet with him.

"What's wrong?" I asked. He was peering ahead of him.

"Bird calls," he said, "where even in the jungle these birds are quiet when groups of men approach. Somone is up ahead." I fell back to the captain and Tamura worked his way into the brush. The captain was giving orders that in case of attack alternate guards should fire at the attackers and the others should kill as many prisoners as possible. In that way, he reasoned, the attackers

101

would have to realize what harm they were doing to their friends and retire.

We slowed almost to a halt and the prisoners quickly realized something was happening. I think they had less hope for rescue than the pleasure of seeing their captors on edge. We moved along for perhaps five minutes. Then from up ahead there came a flat sound like a shot and a shrill scream. The captain didn't move. After a minute, he pointed to the boy guarding him, myself and two guards and ordered us to investigate.

We worked our way cautiously through the brush until I heard a groan. It was Tamura. He lay face down and when he heard me coming up, he raised a finger and pointed at something hung on a bush. I didn't recognize it for what it was until I sniffed at it. It was a firecracker. In sudden understanding, I stood up and ran for Tamura. But he was dead, the victim of a Filipino booby trap. They used a firecracker on a trip device, and lined the surrounding territory with beds of sharpened bamboo stakes. The sound of a shot would send men diving for cover and they would meet their death on the stakes. Tamura's jungle-fighting reflexes had been too good. He moved before he thought.

I went back and told Captain Umara what had happened. It was possible that the trap was old, but it was equally possible that a guerrilla band was in the vicinity. Once darkness came, it wouldn't take much of a diversion to start the prisoners rioting. At this point, they knew that they had little to lose.

Umara realized this and, after checking his maps, decided we could make the rail depot before dusk if we picked up the pace. His orders were passed down the line and our guards went among the Americans with kicks and bayonets and butts to force them into action. We no sooner got them under way when a captive noncommissioned officer approached Captain Umara.

"The men just can't stand the pace," he pleaded. "Can't you allow us a few minutes rest?"

"That would leave us in a bad tactical position, where

your friends are concerned, after dark," the captain answered him. The man listened to my translation.

"We will give some kind of guarantee that we won't try to escape," he started to argue but thought better of it. The captain motioned him back to his men. He refused to move.

"The pace will kill some of them!" he shouted. Umara didn't so much as ask for a translation. He waved the guards to push the man back among the prisoners. The man went and started to pass a word which the others nodded to. I moved in closer and caught what he was saying.

"He is advising a slowdown," I warned Umara. At the captain's command two guards broke the prisoners away from the offender. The Ox walked behind the man with his bayonet pressed against his back.

"Move faster," I told him, translating Umara's orders. The prisoner looked at me and kept his slow step. The Ox moved faster pressing the blade into the man's back. For a brief second, it looked certain that the man would break and move faster. Instead, he drew himself erect and stood his ground. The Ox moved toward him slowly. As we watched, the blade entered the man's back. Suddenly, it showed in the front of his chest. He pitched forward, falling free of the blade. Then he slowly started to his feet and regained them. Umara walked over and blew off part of his head with a big lead bullet from his 9-mm. revolver.

Several prisoners started forward and the guards cut them down with rifle fire. They put down five or six and immediately the Ox was among the fallen men finishing them with his rifle butt. The others turned stricken faces away from the carnage and moved on, the possible rebellion was broken.

We reached our destination some twenty minutes later. Other Imperial troops loaded the prisoners into box cars and our end of the job was done. Umara walked around patting his belly with both hands like a man well satisfied with a large dinner.

"They will not forget us," he kept saying as the many faces turned for a last look at us as they disappeared into the box cars. "They won't forget us," he repeated and laughed.

I wondered if he remembered his words later when he was part of a regiment based on the 5th Division when it was annihilated by American troops on Saipan.

# THE G.I.'S DIED LIKE FLIES AT KASSERINE PASS!

## By Gerhardt Brehn
### Lieutenant, 21st Panzer Division

"LET'S SEE if they know this one," said *Oberkommando* Kleinschimdt, rapidly chalking in arrows on the acetate that hung over the relief map. Then, lighting his cigar, he turned back to us with a thin smile. "You ten tank commanders have the honor of being the first to meet the Americans in combat. I know you'll do well. Dismissed."

We filed out from under the canvas sheet stretched between a radio truck and some gnarled conifers, and headed for our Mark IV's. The crews were already in them, mechanics busy giving them a last-minute check.

"That's the oldest one in the book," grunted Lt. Brugmann.

"Yes, but you have to remember that they've never seen combat before," I answered, swinging myself into the turret. "See you later."

I kept the lid up, resting on my shoulders, enjoying a last quick smoke. The tanks' motors were rumbling smoothly as we waited for the jump-off signal. The *Oberkommando* strolled out of the command post, glanced at his watch and raised one arm. In the distance, I could still hear the monotonous droning and screaming of Stukas, the heavy detonation of bombs and answering ack-ack as the Luftwaffe pounded away at Sidi-bou-Zid, softening it up for us.

Suddenly, the *Oberkommando* dropped his arm.

I tapped the driver's shoulder with my foot and we began to grind slowly forward, dust billowing out from all sides. I saw Brugmann grin at me from his turret, holding up his hand with thumb and forefinger forming a circle, and I waved back.

We reached Point A of the *Oberkommando's* plan—the crest of a cactus-strewn hill overlooking the forward positions of the American 34th Infantry Division—in twelve minutes. We stopped there and calmly surveyed the broad valley and ragged, saw-toothed mountains of the Primary Tunisian Dorsal sixty miles behind them. The Stukas had left, but smoke was still rising from Sidi-bou-Zid, a chill wind blowing it across the American positions.

We knew they could see our tanks outlined against the skyline but nothing happened. Five minutes passed—ten minutes, fifteen. I was beginning to wonder how sound the *Oberkommando's* plan was when I suddenly heard the unmistakable squeak of tank treads. Seconds later. I saw the first of the Shermans come lumbering through the smoke, then another one—and another. There were at least twenty-five of them, all flying the triangular pennants of the U.S. 1st Armored Division.

There was a sharp crack from one of their turret guns, and the scream of a shell. The earth mushroomed up nearby, and rock fragments rained down on us.

"All right! Let's get out of here!" I shouted, slamming the lid down. Expertly, the driver backed us away, swung around and took off. The other tanks were also dividing and falling back. I could hear the grinding of gears, the roar of motors, hear the American shells falling among us—then a new sound. The deadly 'crump' of our 88's. A cheer went up from the crew.

"They walked right into that one!" shouted our gunner.

I swung the turret around and peered out the periscope. The Shermans were pouring over the hill—into an inferno. Three of them were already burning, others exploding in front of my eyes as 88-crews pumped shell after shell into them. They'd had the position zeroed in —there was no escape. As the Shermans hurriedly backed off, the 88-crews, who'd been expecting this, suddenly lifted the range to 400 yards. Armor-piercing shells

106

continued to smash into them, reducing the Shermans to twisted wreckage. We saw some of the crews piling out of them, trying to run for it, heard the rattle of small-arms fire and saw them crumple to the ground.

"My God!" I shouted. "It's like a shooting gallery!"

It was. Exactly. The *Oberkommando* had been right —they *hadn't* known this one. Even though it was one of the oldest tricks in the tank-man's book.

"I don't think we'll have to worry about the Americans, Lieutenant," grinned our gunner. "They're going to be a pushover."

For the past month, we'd all been eager to get a crack at the Americans, to feel them out, test their brains and mettle. But, up to now, the opportunity hadn't arisen. We'd been too busy with Montgomery. Now, however, Rommel had decided to deal with them. He had to. He knew it was only a question of time before the Eighth Army would be striking us again in the south, and he couldn't afford to face one strong force and have another, a complete new army, moving in on his flank.

His plan was to strike first at the inexperienced American troops just building up into a fair-sized combat force in the Faid Sbeitla area, then turn back to meet the attack he knew was coming from Montgomery.

So a few days earlier we'd begun a series of small local attacks from Kairouan south, taking the key mountains on the Secondary Tunisian Dorsal. Then, on January 30, 1943, we'd suddenly struck with tanks at Faid Pass, just west of Sfax, which was being held by the French. Our armor and artillery had cut through their defenses like a hot knife through butter, inflicting heavy casualties. We'd surged through the pass, the momentum of the attack carrying us right to the outskirts of Sidi-bou-Zid, in the plain west of the Dorsal, and Rommel—knowing that American combat teams were stationed there—had decided to put out feelers. Our tank platoon was one of those feelers.

The Americans themselves supplied the other. During the next week they made two attempts to retake the pass, but immediately on coming through it we had concentrated a large quantity of artillery at its mouth and we sent them reeling back both times under a blizzard of steel. In everyone's opinion they were very raw, very inexperienced.

The French had been so badly mauled in the Faid Pass that Giraud withdrew all his forces from the Tunisian front for training and re-equipping with U.S. equipment. This left the Americans stretched out thinly on a ninety-mile 'line' which was actually nothing more than several strong points near the mountain passes that they thought we might use in our push west.

At this point, Intelligence told us that Eisenhower, suddenly concerned by the exposed southeastern flank of his forces in Tunisia, had ordered the 1st Armored Division, the 1st and 34th Infantry Divisions, and units from the 9th Infantry Division, regrouped into one striking force in the plain that separated us from the Primary Dorsal. Realizing how effective such a force could be, Rommel decided to attack before the Allied Commander's orders could be carried out.

February 14th was cold and rainy, with a leaden overcast just scraping the tops of the mountains. A hour before dawn, the earth began to tremble with the rumble of tank treads as Rommel brought 150 of his tanks through three passes in the vicinity of Faid. One group of twenty came directly out of Faid, another fifty out of a pass to the north of Faid, catching the U. S. infantry and artillery at Djebel Lessouda, six miles west of Faid, in the rear. A third group of twenty came out of a pass south of Faid, below Sidi-bou-Zid, while another fifty tanks were held in reserve.

Our advance team of twenty tanks and artillery at the western end of Faid spear-headed the attack on Sidi-bou-Zid while 10th Panzer swept around Gafso towards Kasserine. Between these two pincers, thousands of Americans were to be cut off and captured. Jumping-off in the dark, the rumble of more armor behind us, we filed through rain and mist, our turrets unbuttoned until we reached the crest of the hill outside the town. There we found fifteen Shermans waiting while another twenty-two were on a ridge to the left. We sat there and shot at them, knocking out about five, while we lost three. Then the Shermans began coming over the ridge and turned out to be forty, including four half-tracks mounting 75 mm. cannons.

We fell back rapidly and scattered while crews unlimbered the 88's that every third tank had been hauling. It was all done so fast that the Shermans were still carefully feeling their way down the ridge like fat old ladies when we opened the barrage. The grey-green smoke of the shellbursts clouded the tanks, the clang of armor-piercing shells against metal rang through the hills. The Shermans panicked, twisting this way and that, and one of them actually turned over—but the 75 mms. were getting in their licks with deadly accuracy.

A 52-ton Mark VI from the Second Group of 21st Panzer took a direct hit. The front crumpled in like a paper bag, the treads snapping. It began to burn immediately. Then its ammunition went off. None of the crew got out.

An 88, mounting cannister, tore the crew apart on one of the 75 mms., while six of us Mark IVs filed off. We climbed a rise to the right, our turrets following the half-tracks, and tossing the works at them. Another one went up with a roar of its own ammunition, while a third stood there unmanned. The fourth tank-buster, still in action, continued to raise havoc, but it was careless—it allowed us to out-flank it. We destroyed it in a cross-fire so intense that the treads actually melted.

Back at the bottom of the ridge, our tanks messed it up with the Shermans, using all the tricks, feints and dodgers that we'd learned at El Alamein and Tobruk. They were no match for us although their gunnery was surprisingly accurate. Leaving twelve Mark IV's to deal with them, the rest of the column ground toward Sidi-bou-Zid.

Suddenly, there was a hollow 'crump' up ahead and the lead tank's tread snapped. It pulled off to the side of the road. At first, I thought they'd mined the area but when the tank's turret opened there was a rattle of small-arms fire and the tank commander flopped over

109

the side. Unbuttoning my own turret, I grabbed the machine gun and swivelled it around as we passed. Sure enough, there were three American soldiers crouching in a shallow depression. I gave them a short blast and the grenade they'd just started to toss fell short, taking them up with it.

I moved into the lead, but stayed up on top, gun ready. Through the periscope down below, your vision starts twenty feet from the tank; you're blind to anything closer. Any infantryman with guts can stay low until the tank is less than twenty feet from him, then stand up and toss anything he wants—even a blockbuster. These Americans had probably learned the trick from the British— who, in turn, had learned it from us at El Alamein.

The fighting was thick the rest of the way into town, but the Americans still hadn't learned to cover their infantry. The foot-soldiers, helpless and alone in the open, were cut down by the hundreds.

"It's like swatting flies," was the way our gunner put it.

Sidi-bou-Zid itself was a smoking ruin. We stopped there to regroup, count noses and set up a forward command post. The town had cost us eight tanks, two half-tracks and around eighteen men; defending it had cost the Americans forty tanks, fifteen self-propelled guns, seven half-tracks, an unknown number of casualties and seventy-one prisoners.

News was now leaking in from the rest of the offensive. Our forces had already overrun the U. S. artillery positions at Djebel Lessouda. The rest of the American combat teams in the north had attacked but were beaten back. To the south, the 10th Panzer continued to drive across the plain to the Primary Dorsal, half-hidden by the low-hanging clouds ahead of us.

The next day, the 15th, the Americans on both sides of the pass tried to counterattack from Hajeb el Aioun but their tanks suffered crippling losses when they ran into the 88's that we'd again set up. As the day wore on, they began to withdraw across the plain to Sbeitla. Most of the U. S. troops at Djebel Lessouda got away but they lost all their heavy equipment. A battalion of motorized infantry was lost in its entirety at Djebel Ksaira when we cut it off.

The American combat teams had the same number of tanks and men that we had, but we dealt with each team separately while the U. S. units were too far apart to be quickly regrouped as one force. The powerful U. S. II Corps, 200 tanks strong, might have saved the day, but it was kept out of the battle at Faid because faulty intelligence made it seem like the Faid attack was a diversion for the main assault which would hit farther north at Pichon.

That night, though, the II Corps, realizing their error, headed south to Sbeitla where they were joined by remnants of forces withdrawing from the Faid area. The whole plain was dotted with flaming tanks and vehicles as the U. S. troops retreated on foot.

On the 17th, the Americans got in their first good counterblow at us and our respect for them shot up. They might be green, but they had brains and guts—and were learning fast. We had sent forty tanks rumbling across the plain after them, picking off stragglers, not realizing that another tank outfit had been moved out of reserve and into a place of concealment. The Americans withheld their fire until we were only 600 yards away and then opened a withering fire. It was a beautiful ambush and their gunnery was superb. We lost twenty tanks. The rest of us limped back, licking our wounds.

But that wasn't enough to stop us. We were right on the heels of withdrawing U. S. units. After two attacks, Sbeitla fell and the Americans withdrew into the Kasserine Pass. Our column, with about thirty heavy Mark IV tanks, towing artillery, and about 250 light vehicles, split up and entered the town from two sides.

By nightfall of the 17th, we had taken the towns of Kasserine, Sbeitla and Feriana. There was little activity on the 18th, but we brought up artillery and began shelling the Americans on each side of the pass. The shelling was followed by battle-hardened Panzer Grenadier infantry which infiltrated U. S. lines. Then, at dawn on the 19th, the tanks moved in . . .

111

Getting into the pass was a cinch. Whoever was charged with laying the mine fields at the entrance missed the boat. They were clumsily planted and way out of range of the U. S. artillery—so we just planted red flags to mark the route and ground our way in.

The battle that followed was a one-sided massacre. Despite having the advantage of a naturally strong defensive position in the pass, the Americans buckled and gave way. Inexperienced troops were stampeding one another to get out from under our fire. They were milling about in the open, running in the wrong direction, while their armor, instead of covering them, simply blocked their way and added to the confusion. Our gunners' only job was to get as many of them with as little ammunition as possible, as word had come from the rear that we were running low.

The prisoners we took were all asking each other the same thing: "Where the hell's our air?" For there hadn't been the sound of one plane overhead during the battle. The dense, low-hanging overcast was the answer. Miles back of the firing line, according to our ever-accurate intelligence, the U. S. Twelfth Air Support Command had a medium-sized field crammed with the biggest air armada the U. S. had ever massed in one place in North Africa. Each one of us kept our fingers crossed that the zero ceiling would last.

We broke out of the westward end of the pass, and on February 21st started to move on Thala, where the British line hinged with the American. If Thala fell, the Thala-Tebessa road was open and our tanks could then rush around the rear of the American units and bag them.

A British armored brigade had been hurried down from the north to strengthen the line at this point. It was supported by U. S. artillery from the 9th Infantry Division which had marched 735 miles in less than 100 hours to answer the call for help. Other British armored units were arriving at Sbiba with brand new 48-ton Churchill tanks—never before used in combat.

The battle was a furious one. Despite terrific day and

112

night artillery bombardment, our column smashed to within four miles of Thala on February 21. The following dawn, we heard the drone of planes above the overcast, and the bombs began to fall. Flying weather or not, Spaatz had ordered every plane that could fly into the air. Hour after hour, squadrons of Flying Fortresses, Marauders, Mitchells and Bostons plastered us.

On the ground, taking advantage of the diversion, the Americans moved 105's up into range of Kasserine Pass and pumped more than 2000 shells into us. Rommel himself came forward to look over the situation, and decided that he lacked supplies and transport to push on. Our spearhead column, surrounded by mountains and increasing numbers of Allied troops, was in danger of being cut off. Deciding that he'd taken all the prisoners he could, he sorrowfully ordered withdrawal.

It was a sad moment for all of us. Only four more miles and we could have disposed of the entire American army in North Africa!

It was while fighting desperate rear-guard action, covering the withdrawal of our light vehicles into the pass, that they finally bagged our tank. We were moving along at about 14 m.p.h., the turret swivelled almost completely around, firing steadily at two Shermans and a Churchill which were slowly closing in. Another Sherman came up and we hit it at the same range with one shot. It went through the turret, and the tank blossomed into flame. Then another Sherman approached the burning tank. It was a stupid thing to do, because we only had to bring our gun over a hair, and he flamed too with our first shot.

Then our gun jammed and the remaining tanks closed in. A shell went through our bogie wheels and another hit our turret but didn't penetrate. A few seconds later we were hit in the suspension system. Each shell hitting sounded like the smash of an enormous hammer, making our ears ring.

As soon as we managed to unjam our gun we began firing again, but another shell smashed the bottom of our left rear gas tank, and flaming gasoline spurted over the back of our tank. We started to bail out, everyone making it except our driver. I dropped back down and tried

113

to pull him out, but found he was dead—and how! His body looked like it had been put through a chopper and then burned.

Some American infantrymen rounded us up and marched us back to their command post. On the way we passed Brugmann's tank. It was burning at the side of the road. The rest of the way in, I had to lean on an American infantryman's shoulder.

The column got back through the pass, losing only eighteen tanks, but the Kasserine offensive was the Afrika Korps' last victory. Their days were already numbered. The rest of the story you know . . .

# SAND, STEEL AND BLOOD

## By Major Howard L. Oleck

SHOCK ACTION is the basic aim of tanks in battle. Smashing, shattering, stunning attack is the main idea of any armored unit. Penetration, breakthrough, and a rampaging drive into the enemy rear is the ultimate purpose.

But always, whatever the mission of an armored unit, one emergency rule always holds true. Whatever the assigned mission may be, if enemy tanks are met the enemy tanks get top priority.

The reason for this Standard Operation Procedure (SOP) is simple. Tankers know that enemy tanks may do to their side what they aim to do to the enemy. Therefore enemy tanks must be stopped. And the best answer to a tank attack is a counterattack, *by tanks*. The best way to stop a tank is with another tank.

A good example of this was the wide-open tank against tank fighting in the North African desert in World War II. The German attack at Faid Pass, and the American counterattack, were classics of tank warfare.

On January 30, 1943 the Germans' 21st Panzer Division, newly equipped and freshly reinforced after the great battle of El Alamein, struck at Faid Pass in Tunisia, not far from Sidi-bou-Zid. In the mile-wide pass a small Free French infantry force, desperately holding the bastion on the Allied flank, reeled under the shock of the attack. The veteran German tankmen struck. While one tank column smashed into the pass, another flanking column swung around the northeast corner of the defensive position to hit it from the side.

At the same time, two other spearheads drove forward in wide circling arcs. One looped around the south of the pass, to take Faid Village and cut off escape behind the pass. The other spearhead moved farther south to the high ground of the Djebel (Hill) bou Dzer, to follow up the attack with a breakthrough, or to flank any counterattacking force.

It was a "by-the-book" example of wily, powerful tank attack—a clever example of *Blitzkrieg* tactics. Over the moving iron spearheads, Stuka dive bombers wheeled and circled, diving like black vultures at any strong point that slowed down the steadily advancing tank columns. Behind the tanks, in armored personnel carriers, Panzer Grenadiers (Armored Infantry) rode, ready to aid the tanks or to occupy captured positions.

Northeast of Sidi-bou-Zid lay the American 1st Armored Division, at Sbeitla. Urgent calls for help flashed to it from the hopelessly outclassed French unit in Faid Pass. The American division, still green, and still mostly untried, was ordered to counterattack.

"Stop the Nazi spearheads!" were the instructions.

Combat Command A (CC/A) of the 1st Armored, led by Brig. Gen. Raymond McQuillin, moved out of bivouac, and started its steel column of roaring, clanking machines towards the east. As evening fell, this column halted near the western end of Faid Pass while reconnaissance scout cars moved gingerly forward, feeling for the enemy.

At the same time Combat Command C (CC/C) started forward, led by Col. Robert I. Stack, east of the Sidi-bou-Zid area. This column was to hit any advancing enemy force on its flank at Maizila Pass south of Faid Pass, and to stop it with a head-on smash, or by crossing the "T."

Tank tactics in open country are like naval tactics. Each side tries to "Cross the T." That means that each column wants to cut directly across the line of advance of the enemy column. That way, the crossing column's tanks can concentrate their fire on the leading enemy tank, and pound it to death. The outmaneuvered column finds that its own tanks are in its line of fire, and they interfere with each other.

A third counterattack column from 1st Armored Division, Combat Command D (CC/D) led by Brig.

116

Gen. Robert Maraist headed south too. It moved through Gafsa, over eighty miles below Faid Pass, to attack Sened and Sened Station while the Germans were busy. That way, it could seize a valuable base, and threaten to make a huge flanking run from the south. CC/B remained behind, in reserve.

That was the "big picture" plan of the Americans. Next step was the actual, close-in "tactical" clash.

At three o'clock in the morning of January 31, McQuillin sent a tank force led by Col. Alex Stark to meet the advancing Panzers at the western exit from Faid Pass. Another group (Task Force Kern) was to swing a little south, and hit the main enemy advance from that direction.

Stark's Task Force had hoped to move up a trail above Faid, and then swarm down into the pass where the French unit had been obliterated.

But the Germans had not been idle during the night. They had made hasty but formidable preparations for the oncoming American counterattack.

Minefields had been sewn in the area where the hill rises began. In the pass itself several German tanks had been placed behind rocks and in hollows, in defilade, with their guns aimed west.

Panzer Grenadiers had dug in below the slope and on it, in foxholes, and slit trenches. Heavy anti-tank guns (the deadly 88's) had been skillfully sited on the slopes. Heavy machine guns and mortars also had been emplaced. From the hillsides, they had perfect observation.

The German plan was to hold the hill masses on both sides of the pass in a solid grip. Then, through the pass, the Panzer columns could strike out like coiled snakes, led by huge Tiger Tanks. In the morning the columns of Nazi armor started to move east, out of the pass. Any American counterattack was bound to suffer heavily from the concealed anti-tank guns, as well as from the Panzers themselves.

Stark's column advanced toward the pass. Company H, First Armored Regiment, led the dangerous counterattack against the ominous hills and pass.

Stark ordered the 91st Armored Field Artillery Battalion to halt its self-propelled guns just within good range of the pass. Accompanying armored infantry carriers followed the tanks.

Then, one by one, the attacking tanks ran into just about every possible enemy defensive device. First was a minefield. Continuing in column, the tanks passed through the deadly zone in single file. Fortunately no tank had its tracks broken by the light anti-personnel mines. Column formation is best for passing through a minefield. Each tank follows the path of the one ahead of it. Cracking eruptions of the land mines, that would have torn a man to pieces, did not halt the big M4 Shermans.

Once through the minefield, the tanks shifted into line for attack, as small arms fire from Kraut infantry began to drum on their armor. In a long assault wave they rolled forward, right over the foxholes. This was shock assault against infantry—a cinch for tanks. Behind the machines, armored infantrymen followed, to capture or finish off those Nazis who did not break and run. So far, so good.

Beyond the light infantry defense line, the tanks shifted formation again. This time they moved in V formation— a line of V's—five tanks (one platoon) in each V. From this this formation they could most quickly shift into either line, column, or echelon.

Near the foot of the first hill, a storm of German anti-tank gun fire blazed out at the approaching V's. Normally, tanks avoid running up so close to dominating positions where AT guns are likely to be concealed. But the mission called for it, and they moved forward. From the turrets of the Shermans their 75's spat back at the 88's concealed in groves of trees up on the slope.

Once a strong enemy position is located, tank tactics call for a basic maneuver called "fire and movement." One group of tanks (two tanks out of a five-tank platoon; or one platoon out of a three-platoon company) stop, and form the "base of fire."

The "base of fire" tanks take defilade position, if there is any cover behind which to halt. In "defilade," only the tank's turret and gun are exposed to enemy fire, while the hull is hidden by the rise of earth in front. If no cover is available, the "base of fire" tanks

118

simply stop, or slow down. Then they can fire more accurately. Their job is to engage the enemy in a firefight, while the other tanks move up.

The "movement" group usually swings around the enemy position in order to attack it from the flank. But at Faid Pass the whole hill mass was full of enemy guns and troops. More important, the mission of the Task Force was not to get involved in aimless fights. Its job was plain—to stop the exit from Faid Pass, put a cork in the bottleneck, and stop the threatened drive of German Panzer columns out.

So, while a platoon of mediums stopped, and dueled with the AT guns up the hill, the other platoons ranged themselves into a new formation—echelon formation, heading south towards the exit from the pass.

In echelon formation, all tanks could fire straight ahead, towards the pass, without blocking each other. At the same time, by turning their turrets to the left they could fire at the AT guns on the hill. Also, if one tank is hit and stopped in an echelon movement, it does not block the advance of the others. They close up the gap and keep moving.

Just so, the counterattacking column raked the hillside to the east as it went by, rolling south. At the same time they called back to their artillery, over their radios, for bombardment of the hill positions. Once artillery fire started to pound the AT positions on the hill, the tanks could concentrate on the pass.

At that moment, the Panzer columns started to emerge from the pass. In two parallel columns, the big German tanks streamed out towards the plain. Like two fleets at sea, the two hostile groups of fighting machines approached each other.

A deadly race began—the stakes were literally victory or death. The one that managed to cross the "T" of the other would have a fearful advantage.

Dust and smoke boiled up as the spinning tracks kicked up sand on the hard ground. The plain and pass reverberated with the shattering roars of powerful engines and the hellish clatter of tortured steel. That most terrible of all modern war's spectacles was about to begin

—the clash of tanks against tanks, steel against steel, *in an earthshaking battle of giants.*

Inside the tanks, sweating men strained to push big shells up to steaming cannon. Drivers pulled open throttles on engines already bellowing at full speed. Tank commanders peered through periscopes and snapped ranges and fire commands to their gunners. One after another, in both groups of tanks, the big guns began to crack and roar.

The American commander spoke quietly into his radio mike. "Shift formation! All tanks change formation! Take column formation!"

The echelon shifted into a column, as the tanks rocked and lurched ahead. All guns started to bear left, straight at the approaching Panzer columns.

In the German tanks, cold sweat beaded the brows of the tank commanders. The American Shermans were faster. The Americans were going to cut right across the Nazi columns—*to cross the "T."* Frantic calls for help crackled back to the Luftwaffe planes.

The planes came swiftly. *But it was too late.* Right across—in front of the Panzer columns, the racing Shermans streamed. Their 75's raked the big German tanks as they passed. One after another the Panzers shuddered and veered as armor piercing shells smashed into them. Then the Panzer columns turned hastily, and wheeled around, back towards the pass. Behind them they left the flaming wrecks of their tanks.

In the triumphant American column, shells struck the Shermans too. Disabled tanks cluttered the field.

Overhead, Messerschmitt ME-109's darted, strafing the armored infantry behind the tanks—preventing the GI's from storming into the pass. Then JU-87's came over, bombing and machine gunning the Americans, forcing the supporting artillery to take cover.

The Shermans were unharmed by the air attack. But without their supporting infantry and artillery they would have been mad to enter the pass in pursuit. The column turned away, and rolled back west.

"Mission accomplished!" Radio messages flashed back to the Division Command Post. *The Panzers had been stopped*—at a price. Several American tanks were lost —but they had been victorious nevertheless. Every trick in the book had been used—every tactical formation—in the wild battle. The Panzers had been beaten.

The story was much the same in all the three Combat Commands. The German advance was stopped.

Far to the south, CC/D swung around Sened, beat off the Germans there, and captured Sened Station. At Maizila Pass, in another swirling run, CC/C cut right across the exit from that pass, turning back the Panzer column that tried to burst out.

In the south, the defeated Nazis pulled back to Maknassy to lick their wounds. At Maizilla Pass and Faid Pass they backed into their prepared positions. Their dream of a smashing breakthrough had ended.

It was not a full victory. The Americans had advanced only at Sened, and not at the two passes. *But they had met and frustrated the best the Afrika Corps and Panzer columns could throw at them.*

Even more important, the Americans had tested and proved their tank tactics in the fiery crucible of battle. Every formation and maneuver laid down in their training manuals was proved to be sound. In the open battleground of North Africa's deserts and hills, the tactics of the GI's had won out over the tough, experienced German desert tank columns that had terrorized the world.

From these battles the Yanks garnered the sure "know-how" that eventually would win the greatest war in history. At the cost of burning tanks and dead and wounded men—the inevitable price of war—they learned once and for all *"how to do it."*

So ended the greatest German tank attack of Faid Pass, under the smashing counterattack of an American tank column. The war was still far from over. But the Americans were on the right track, in terms of men, equipment, and tactics—*and they knew it.*

Tanks against tanks, the Americans knew that they could take on, and lick, *any enemy in the world.*

# IT TOOK MORE THAN
# GUTS: IWO JIMA!

### By C. L. Morehead

FOR EVERY NATION there is a standard of bravery in battle. For the French, perhaps the defense of Verdun in World War I is the standard. For the British, perhaps the stubborn, orderly evacuation of Dunkirk. For the American, there can be little doubt.

It was Iwo Jima.

On Iwo Jima the American standard reached a peak. That is why the immortal photo of the "Flag Raising On Mt. Suribachi" touched the heart of every American.

On the black sands of Iwo Jima, early in 1945, 4300 United States Marines died, and 15,308 were wounded in frontal assaults on a solid mass of hidden forts. The Marines killed 23,000 fanatical Japanese defenders, who fought to the death, there. Less than 100 prisoners were taken, and they were almost all stunned or wounded men.

Surely Americans do not want to die. Life in the U.S.A. is good. Yet, when they are challenged, they seem to fight with deadly efficiency. It may be that the Marine motto, simple as it is, expresses the real reason why.

*Semper Fidelis* means "Always Faithful." Faithful to what? To the American dream. To freedom, to justice, to the dignity of the individual.

And there it is—the dignity of the individual. If a man is to have self-respect and dignity, he must be ready to fight for his principles.

And to die for them.

At Iwo Jima it was all "individuals." No mass "*banzai* charges," no "human sea," no cattle-like charges, for

122

Americans. Each man advanced against concrete pillboxes, through storms of flying steel and flame, as an individual, because of ideals and because of pride.

That is how it is with most Americans, especially in the Marines. They are not supermen. They know the sweating fear of combat. They too shrink from the tearing, ripping steel and shattering explosions of battle. But they choke down their fear, and go forward, because a free man must.

Take Private Mike Morse, of New York City, for example. He was not a hardened veteran when he landed on Iwo Jima. Less than six months before, he had joined up. After boot training he was shipped right out to Guam, for a few weeks more of training. Then, off he went, with the 21st Marines, in the 3rd Marine Division, to the most brutal fight in American history.

In the murderous, face to face clawing of "Cushman's Pocket," Mike fought his first battle. In a rocky, stand-strewn space not much bigger than a football field, he inched his way with his buddies, through a crazy network of pillboxes and blockhouses. From three-foot-thick concrete walls, almost invisible muzzles of Mambu machine guns and cannon spat death at him. From skillfully hidden cave holes, darting Japs hurled grenades that smashed the black rubber near him. The ground seemed to heave and convulse. Roaring noise and smoke enveloped him.

Mike crawled and slithered through the shattered earth and debris. When he saw a flitting Jap figure he fired his carbine, or flung a grenade. The hours melted into days of thundering chaos, dead bodies, blood, and cold sweat. Over it all rain beat down, soaking and chilling him.

When his battalion was ordered back for a brief rest, Mike lay on the wet sand in the "rear," exhausted like the other men. The "rear" was a grim joke. Shell, mortar, and machine gun fire slammed down into the "rest area."

That was why he was almost glad when he was called to help carry the wounded back to the beach for evacuation. It was better to be doing something. Almost tenderly he picked his way over the broken ground, carrying a stretcher with a still, grey-faced man on it.

123

The shell burst that hit him struck while he was carrying a particularly badly wounded Marine. Flying shrapnel smashed into Mike's face, around his eyes. Blood spurted, cascading into his eyes, and running warmly down his cheek.

Blinking, he peered through the red mist, and wiped the back of one grimy hand across his face. But stubbornly he held onto the stretcher. He would not let the wounded man fall.

Staggering, half-blinded, his face streaming with gore, Mike kept going, until he delivered his wounded charge to the evacuation point. Only then would he think of his own wounds.

Mike would have been surprised and embarrassed to be called a hero.

A man did what he had to do, on Iwo Jima.

Almost every inch of the black, ugly island was torn up by shell bursts. Volcanic grit blew into men's faces, when the rain was not soaking it. Dead bodies littered the barren ground, and drifts of black sand piled up in dunes half-covering them. The dunes blended with the hundreds of slight mounds that dotted the island. Each tiny mound marked one of the hundreds of buried, tunnel-connected fortress pillboxes.

Sergeant Robert P. Fowler, of Washington, D. C., met a Jap, almost face to face, as both crawled towards each other. The Jap flung a grenade, and then dodged behind a rock as Fowler first ducked under the burst, then fired at the edge of the rock. The Jap slithered back behind another rock.

After him came Fowler, crawling with his carbine cradled in his arms. When he caught a glimpse of the slithering legs or helmet of his enemy, he fired quickly. Around the broken rocks the deadly duel went on. Shot after shot spanged low across the ground.

It was the American who won.

The moment came when the target was visible for a split second. In that moment the American's trigger squeeze was an eyewink surer and quicker, and his bullet snuffed out the life of his enemy.

It was kill or be killed on Iwo. All over the hellish

124

island these murderous little duels swirled and crackled.

PFC John MacElroy, of Williamsport, Pennsylvania, had teamed up with another rifleman to smash a pillbox with grenades and satchel charges. Then he scraped a hole in the sand nearby, and slept in it through the night.

At dawn his partner awoke and began to clean his gun. From the shattered pillbox a shot rang out. Mac-Elroy's buddy fell dead. One of the pillbox crew, still alive, was determined to die fighting. He did too, burned to a horrible cinder by a flamethrower in the renewed attack on his broken little fortress.

Insanely tenacious, almost every single one of the island's garrison had to be killed in close combat. Sometimes it seemed that each one had to be killed twice. Repeatedly, areas that were thought to be solidly secured, even in the rear, burst into renewed and venomous life. Through a maze of underground tunnels the defenders filtered back and forth throughout the island.

Second Lt. Frank J. Wright, of Pittsburgh, Pennsylvania, hit the beach with sixty men in his platoon. In one and a half hours of fighting, only two men remained able to move with him. They were PFC Remo Bechelli, of Detroit, Michigan, PFC Lee Zuck, of Scranton, Pennsylvania. He had been ordered to rush across the narrow neck of the island next to Mt. Suribachi, and isolate the hill, and he did just that. Four of his company's officers, including his company commander, were killed as they followed him. When he reached the other side, Wright was the company commander.

"We weren't trying to run a foot race," he said, "but our orders were to get across the island as fast as possible, and that's what we did."

A very matter-of-fact point of view. But that is the Yank's point of view about war. It is just a dirty, nasty job, that has to be done. So he does it as quickly and efficiently as he can—to get it over with.

When Second Lt. Norman Brueggman, of Akron, Ohio, leaped to lead a charge of his platoon up a slope, he put this viewpoint into words. His men were momentarily paralyzed by the smashing, raking fire from

125

above. His exasperation bellowed out: "If you want to win this war you'd better get the hell up here."

Lt. Col. Charles E. Shepard, of La Jolla, California, C.O. of a battalion of the 28th Marines, put it this way. He explained the mission to his men as a double job: "One, to secure this lousy piece of real estate so we can get the hell off it. Two, to help as many Nips as possible to keep their oath to die for the Emperor."

Equally typical was the American zest for collecting souvenirs. Many a Yank risked his life for a souvenir.

PFC Leo Jez, of Chicago, Illinois, collected his trophy, a Samurai sword, the hard way. When a Jap officer came charging out, swinging his sword, Jez leaped forward and grappled with him. As the sword swung down toward him, Jez stopped the glittering blade with his bare hand. Then he wrenched the weapon out of the Jap's hands, and with one terrific swing, slashed the Jap's head off.

His own hand was split deeply, but Jez had the sword —a perfect souvenir.

Scouts and patrols were useless. The lines of attackers and defenders were locked in close contact from the beginning until the end. For almost four weeks the deadly grenade, flame, gun-butt, and knife fighting went on under a deluge of crashing, smashing mortar and shell bursts. Surely, no vision of hell could have matched this awful panorama, where thousands of merciless men tore at each other's throats in a landscape like that of a dead planet.

Here and there, on the rocky, scarred ground, squat tanks of the Third Tank Battalion slid and ground slowly forward. Volleys of anti-tank gun fire smashed into them, and from their turrets streams of flame belched out, into cave entrances and pillbox slits. Major Holly H. Evans, of Oil City, Texas, their commander, admitted grimly, "They knocked the hell out of us for a while." By the second day only nineteen of his forty-six tanks were still usable.

But the fear and hatred of the Japs for the tanks was very real. Many a Nipponese was roasted alive by their flamethrowers, or buried alive as the big tank guns smashed the caves into sealed tombs.

As the inferno roared, day after day, and night after night, it consumed the units. Cooks and clerks, legal officers and MP's, volunteered, or were sent to fill the gaping holes in the slowly advancing lines. PFC Waren K. Gray, of Ewing, Kentucky, a cook, pleaded for a chance to fight.

"He had to be allowed into the lines when it looked for a while as if there would be no one left to cook for." For two days and nights Gray served as mortar fire spotter. At least two dozen Japs were seen to fall under the mortar bursts he directed.

Battle madness grew among the men. Things that would have sickened them at home became matters for bellowing laughter here. When they saw a terrified Jap running out of the door of a pillbox, with a Marine thrusting a bayonet at his backside, the roar of laughter was like that of demons. And when another Marine shot the fleeing Nip, thus depriving the pursuer of his game, the black field rang with hysterical laughter.

The same insane kind of humor came from the Japs. When a charging Marine, holding a grenade in his hand, was hit on the edge of a trench, he stood swaying for an instant before he fell. When he fell upon his own grenade, and was blown to pieces, the screaming cackles of the invisible Japs told of their enjoyment of the sight.

In the bedlam, many men lost much of their ordinary sense of caution. First Lt. Felix Edico, of the Bronx, New York, ran up to a Jap tank and rolled grenades down its gun barrel.

Second Lt. Charles Little, of Arcadia, California, set up an artillery forward observer post in a shell hole surrounded by dead bodies. But the bodies were not dead and grenades suddenly began to fly into his hole. As fast as they came in, he pitched them out again. For half an hour the weird ball game continued, until all the Japs really were dead bodies.

The journal of Major Frank Garretson, of Seattle, Washington, recorded his battalion's moves like the play-by-play story of a mad game. Garretson had starred on the Washington University football team, and he wrote as

127

the companies moved: "We have moved up one touchdown" (100 yards); or "one first down" (10 yards).

Second Lt. Richard Reich, of Oklahoma City, Oklahoma, had joined Company E of the 24th Regiment just before it moved out for the Iwo Invasion. After two days of battle he was a company commander—all the other officers were dead. Promotion was very quick on Iwo. So was the mortality rate.

Battle fatigue became common as nerves broke under the endless strain. Jitters and uncontrollable shaking seized many men. For no special reason a man would begin to retch and vomit. Diarrhea racked the men, leaving them weak and sick. By the third week casualties had become appalling. Each man felt that he would be the next. One company commander lasted just six minutes before he was killed. Buck sergeants were in command of what was left of platoons.

On March 16, twenty-five days after the first landing, the Americans reached the far end of the island at Kitano Point. It was just in time. They could not have stood much more.

Organized, coordinated resistance was ended. But it was to be several days more before the stubborn pockets of trapped Nipponese were to be finally wiped out.

Methodically, the Marines sealed shut every cave and tunnel entrance with flame throwers and dynamite. Canyons were flooded with gasoline, and set aflame. Bulldozers buried pillboxes. Bitter-end resistance continued from isolated nests and single survivors, who had to be killed one by one. Many an American died in this process, after the island had been officially declared "secure."

In many underground caves, the defeated Japanese blew themselves up, or solemnly committed *hara-kiri*.

Among the exhausted, grim Marines there was no jubiliation. They respected the courage of the fighting men whom they had conquered. Besides, it was hard to rejoice when so many friends had fallen in the battle. The dull eyes and lined faces of the survivors told how they felt.

It had been a hard, bitter job. Thank God, it was done and over.

Only gradually did the realization of what they had done come over the tired men. As they walked about the desolate island, the enormity of its strength became apparent.

In a typical area about 600 by 1000 yards in size, there were 1500 forts, including 225 pillboxes and 268 caves, honeycombed with connecting tunnels. In many places the underground galleries were in three levels, with interlocking tunnels running at all angles from one to another.

The old young men looked at each other in silent wonder. They had conquered this enormous fortress. It was almost incredible.

It began to dawn upon them that they had set a new standard for Americans at war. Beside this, the proud standards of Bunker Hill, Gettysburg, the Argonne, and Normandy became not lower—but surpassed. They had made history. With their blood.

In the days and years to come Americans will always remember Iwo Jima. They will never forget.

Iwo was not in vain. It helped to end the second great World War. But, far more important, it showed what Americans can do, when they have to.

# THE WORLD'S BIGGEST BATTLE

### By Major Howard Oleck

HALF A MILLION Americans were in the greatest single battle in the history of the world—and never knew it. Many of them thought it was just a long ride. Some of them thought it was just a running skirmish. A few of them met death in it, and discovered too late that it was in deadly earnest. A few knew it as just another grim combat. But to most of them it was only a long and confusing tank or truck ride.

Centuries from now, historians will pore over the records of The Battle of the Ruhr with fascinated attention. It was the greatest battle in history.

In it, in 1945, armies of millions clashed and maneuvered, with one enveloping and utterly destroying the other, to end the most titanic war the world had ever seen.

Probably never again will such vast armies meet and lock in mortal combat. The atom bomb has made such enormous concentrations far too dangerous ever to be used again.

The Battle of The Ruhr was planned in 1942, and fought three years later, in 1945. The invasions of North Africa, Italy, and France by the Americans and British, long before, were only preliminaries to this final battle for civilization. The ultimate decision of World War II had to be at the Ruhr, and it had to be planned and prepared for years in advance.

The reason for it was plain from the beginning. The Ruhr was—and is—the industrial heart of Europe, and of Germany. It had to be conquered if Germany was to be conquered.

Back in 1942, while Britain rocked under the smashing attacks of the Luftwaffe, planning for the final defeat of the Nazi empire began. British and American leaders agreed that only invasion of the continent, and destruction of Germany's industrial heart, could win the war.

At the Casablanca Conference, in January 1943, detailed planning began. To head the Allied planning staff, Roosevelt and Churchill selected Lt. General Sir Frederick Morgan, of the British Army. He was to be the Chief of Staff to a Supreme Allied Commander who had not yet been selected. His title itself told what he was to be and do. It was the imposing and suggestive COSSAC (Chief of Staff, Supreme Allied Commander).

COSSAC, and his assistants in the great planning rooms in London, drew up the great master plan for the invasion of France—*Operation Overlord*. The Overlord plan set forth, in precise detail, the invasion itself (the Neptune plan), the many diversionary (cover) plans, and the ultimate battle itself, the battle to isolate and overrun the arsenal fortress of the Ruhr.

Lying just east of the Rhine, the great complex of factories and mines known as The Ruhr resembles the Pittsburgh area of America, plus Detroit and other industrial cities, all gathered into one sixty-by-seventy-mile concentration. It is bounded by the Rhine on the west, the Sieg River on the south, and the Lippe River on the north. In it are the great steel and manufacturing centers of Essen, Dortmund, Duisburg, Wuppertal, Dusseldorf, Solingen and Hagen. Deprived of these sources of armaments, Germany would be unable to wage war. Air bombing could weaken this area, but could never completely destroy its might.

From the initial landings in Normandy, the grand plan drawn up by General Morgan aimed for a long drive northeast to the Ruhr. Then it called for a huge double envelopment battle, to cut off, surround, and liquidate the Ruhr. Berlin was the final target. The Supreme Allied Commander, whoever he might be, was to execute this predetermined plan.

Two thousand years ago, at the battle of Cannae, the perfect double envelopment and destruction of an army had been illustrated in all its terrible effectiveness.

131

Then, the great Carthaginian general Hannibal had surrounded the Roman army and slaughtered it. Now, in this plan, the same tactics were to be used, but on a scale that would have made Hannibal gasp.

Just so, in truth, it happened.

On March 24, 1945, the American Army stood on the west bank of the Rhine, looking across at the Ruhr. General Eisenhower, the Supreme Allied Commander, was ready to execute the decisive steps in General Morgan's grand plan—the seizure of the Ruhr.

With the Americans, north of the Ruhr and above Wesel, were the British and Canadian armies, under Montgomery. South, below Remagen, other American Armies, under Patton, were poised for advance. Fate had smiled upon the Allies, and had given them a great prize of good luck at Remagen. There, the capture of the Ludendorf Bridge, intact, had allowed the Americans to seize a foothold on the east bank of the Rhine.

In the Ruhr area, the core of the Germany army waited, at bay. Commanded by Field Marshal Model, twenty-one German divisions and 325,000 veteran troops braced for the show-down battle.

Against this force, Eisenhower launched not mere divisions but whole armies. On the north near Wesel, the Ninth Army, under General Simpson was ordered to cross the Rhine and drive straight east to Lippstadt and Paderborn. On the south, the First Army, under General Hodges, was to move east from Remagen and Linz in a great sweep, turning north to meet the other spearhead at Lippstadt or Paderborn. Between them they were to catch the German forces in a huge iron embrace.

The new American Fifteenth Army, under General Gerow, was to hold the west bank of the Rhine, threaten the whole western border of the Ruhr, and prevent counterattack.

On the cold, grey morning of March 25th, the attack began. The earth trembled as massed artillery of Corps and Armies volleyed a rain of high explosives across the Rhine. Whole divisions of tanks and infantry swarmed

132

forward, in a tide of armed might that covered the earth.

In the defense lines, Model, the German commander, despite the advantages of powerful defensive positions on familiar ground, made a fatal mistake. Expecting a drive north from the American units already across the Rhine at the Remagen bridgehead, he shifted his forces to meet it. This left almost nothing to stop the drive of the First Army straight east. The attack from Remagen went east, not north.

In the north, the evil "intuition" of the Feuhrer, Hitler, dictated an even more fatal mistake. Seeing his "Thousand Year Reich" crumbling before his eyes, he forbade any withdrawals of units, on pain of death. Forbidden to concentrate his vast army, Field Marshal Model had to leave the scattered German units in the north where they were.

Literally leaping across the Rhine with an airborne attack, Ninth Army smashed into the Germans in the north. In one day, swarming Yank infantry in assault boats crossed the Rhine, built a pontoon bridge at Wesel, and launched armored spearheads east. The largest double envelopment in history was under way.

The southern claw of the pincer moved east almost unopposed. The northern claw ran into one desperate defense after another. All were in vain.

Terrifically powerful and effective, the Americans were deadly efficient at the business of war, by this time. Armored units quickly engaged the defenders, pinned them down for the infantry to strangle, and swept around them in swift loops, isolating them quickly for their inevitable destruction.

As each spearhead sped east, day after day, it detached a division here and there. These were the killer divisions, all aimed at the heart of the Ruhr. Their function was to split up the scattered defensive units, surround them, and wipe them out one by one.

After the first two days of quick advance, stop-and-fight, and advance again, the pace of the two attacking armies became swift. By the third day their tank spearheads were rolling headlong towards their target. Especially the southern claw of the pincers was moving rapidly, wheeling north to meet the other claw.

On April 1st, one week after the jump-off, the two spearheads linked at Lippstadt. The trap was closed.

Inside the trap was an enormous force, now completely surrounded and cut off. Model's command, German Army Group B, contained the Fifth Panzer Army, Fifteenth German Army, and elements of German Army Group H's First Parachute Army. In the trapped enemy force were seven corps, nineteen divisions, and over 100,000 anti-aircraft soldiers, totaling nearly a third of a million men. Twenty-four generals and an admiral were there too.

Bewildered and hopeless, the Germans fought uncertainly and ineffectually as the methodical American killer divisions knifed into their positions. Food and ammunition supplies dwindled. By April 14th the Germans had been crowded into two main pockets of resistance.

From the megalomaniac Hitler came the order to break out of the pockets. In the beleaguered Ruhr the Nazi chiefs simply ignored it. It was futile and meaningless. Only the crashing American shells, grinding tanks, and grim-faced GI's were real now.

Among the avenging Yanks the usual excitement and anger of battle grew to a murderous fury. Their headlong advance had brought them to the German horror factories, concentration camps, and human incinerator plants. Hardly believing their eyes, they beheld one horror after another. The grisly *kultur* of the arrogant German Supermen was exposed for the world to see for the first time.

Nauseated, and half-crazed with loathing and disgust, the GI's flung themselves at the German troops. Now the Yanks fought like avenging spectres, pale-faced with icy rage, and swift and cunning with months and years of battle experience. Before these tigerish killers, the German veterans recoiled in startled fear.

On the roads, behind the racing American assault columns, millions of liberated slaves poured out of the factories and concentration camps. French, Dutch, Belgian, Italian, Czech, Polish, and most of all Russian, the freed slaves wandered, as if by instinct, west to liberty. It was something out of the Dark Ages, the breaking up of a medieval slave state. And here and there the driving attack column found and freed stockade camps full of pale prisoners of war.

Blandly, German PW's and civilians denied that they knew anything about the slave and torture camps all around them. Led to the mass graves and human incinerators, and questioned, they shrugged their shoulders unconcernedly. It was all a matter of orders, they explained. That made it all right. They felt no guilt about it at all.

Hard-faced Americans stared at the Germans with an anger and contempt that verged on murder. Then the GI's turned away, leaving the pitiful piles of scrawny corpses, and the well-fed, self-righteous Germans. It was no use. There was no shame or regret in the nation of murderers-by-order.

At least the Yanks could vent some of their fury on the armed troops in grey still in the Ruhr pockets. Savagely the liberators attacked the isolated Nazi units.

Inside the surrounded German Army, units disintegrated with increasing speed. With utter defeat staring at them, the Germans fumbled for a way to avoid formal surrender. Field Marshal Model had a solution. On April 17th he announced that German Army Group B was dissolved. The men were dismissed and told to try to make their way out, by any means they could find.

Thus Model avoided the responsibility of a surrender. Then he committed suicide.

On the morning of April 18th, organized resistance in the Ruhr ended. The Americans quietly moved in, herded their droves of prisoners into temporary PW camps, and occupied the area.

Three weeks ago the vast attack had begun; now the Allied Armies were running loose all over Germany. In two weeks more the war would be over.

In the joy of final victory, the free world paid little heed to the great Battle of the Ruhr. The link-up with the Russians on the Elbe, the suicide of Hitler, and the end of the world's nightmare were enough to dominate all attention. What was one battle more or less—even if it

135

happened to be the greatest battle of all time! The world was surfeited with, and sick of battles and killing.

The battle for the Ruhr, however enormous it was, was only an episode in the defeat of Germany. It was a tactical victory second to none in history. But it had a significance of far greater importance to the world, in a very different respect.

Ironically, the military meaning of this tactical victory was to blind the free world to its far more vital political meaning. The tactical plan of General Morgan, and the tactical operation of General Eisenhower, completely hid the political effect of this enormous feat of arms.

Engrossed in battle victory, the Americans forgot completely that battle is not the ultimate purpose of war, but is only a means to an end. The American Chiefs of Staff left it all up to Eisenhower.

The politically more experienced British pleaded for the Americans to by-pass the Ruhr, and to dash on to Berlin and the border countries. That had been the master plan. But Eisenhower was more interested in quick battle victory and saving American lives. He had changed the master plan's target, and had told the Russians so. After that, the Americans were committed, and there was no choice.

Had he followed the British advice, the American armies might have overrun Berlin, Czechoslovakia and many other areas now in Communist hands. Perhaps the whole post-war period of "Cold War" with Russia might have been very different. But almost surely many more Yanks would have died in the additional fighting that would have meant.

In executing "the largest double envelopment in history," Eisenhower the general triumphed over Eisenhower the statesman. He chose battle victory and saving of American lives, over political advantage to America. Only God, and the future, know whether or not he was right.

Be that as it may, the Battle of the Ruhr wrote a mighty message on the pages of history. Here in America, it said, is the greatest military force of all time. Let

136

all who dream of conquest read this message, and draw back from war with this guardian of freedom. Let all who would seek to tyranize and enslave recall the charred and blackened shell that became what was once the mighty Ruhr and know that America stands always ready to join her might with that of all liberty-loving men.

# HOLD THAT LINE . . . OR DIE

### By Mitchell Dana

OKINAWA was "the last battle" of World War II. It was the last battle, in truth, for many a man and many a ship and plane. But for the destroyermen of the United States it was a nightmare come true. What the destroyermen took, and what they dished out there, seems unbelievable now.

Okinawa was the last, insanely reckless struggle of the crashing Japanese Empire. In one final burst of teeth-grinding fury, Japan's Suicide Squadrons literally hurled themselves at the Americans. And to stop this maniacal burst of desperation, the burden fell on a long, thin screen of destroyers.

It was men who wanted to live against men who wanted to die. Men in thin-skinned, skittering little "cans" against men in swift-hurtling planes, rockets and torpedoes. And, almost incredibly, it was the men in the little ships who won. Pure skill, bulldog tenacity, and death-defying bravery won out. Men who were too proud to run defeated men who were determined to die.

There were many good little ships in the picket line that surrounded bloody Okinawa. Many good men in them, too. Men like Shipfitter Art Ehrman of the doomed *Abele,* who dove off a rescue ship to save two drowning buddies, when he himself had just been fished out. And men like Water Tender First Class Pete Branigan of the *Lalley,* who stayed at his post shutting off valves on burst steamlines while live steam scorched his skin off.

It would be hard to say "*This* ship and crew was better than *that* one" in the stubborn line. But there was one destroyer that somehow symbolized the spirit of all the gallant "small boys" of the American fleets. *U.S.S. Had-*

*ley* somehow typified the skill and unconquerable fighting spirit of all Yankee destroyermen.

Destroyer *U.S.S. Hugh W. Hadley* had been commissioned in November 1944. She was the latest thing in swift surface ships when she headed west with her new crew. DD 774 was her battle number. Commander B. J. Mullaney was her skipper when she underwent her ordeal by fire in April and May of 1945. Her men were to win a Presidential Unit Citation then, in an unparalleled series of blazing life-or-death battles. But twenty-eight of them were destined to die in the flaming holocaust, and sixty-seven to be burned and torn in the howling hell of the Kamikazes. The *Hadley* herself was to emerge a shattered, staggering wreck.

The Kamikazes were the reason for the bloody, fire-seared chaos off Okinawa. To Americans, to whom the individual and his life are sacred, the Japanese Kamikaze seems an insane horror produced by diseased minds. Not so to the fatalistic Nipponese.

Suicide weapons had been tried before, but never on the horrible scale of Okinawa. Japan's Imperial Navy had secretly launched a whole *Kikusui* plan, using a new "Special Attack Corps" of suicide volunteers. The Kamikaze (Divine Wind) plan was well under way as 1945 began. By March some 190 Japanese pilots, sworn to seek death, already had crashed about 130 planes into American ships, and almost sixty more into the sea in near misses.

Often dressed in ceremonial *hara kiri* (ritual suicide) robes, insanely fanatic Japanese pilots flew the Kamikaze planes, or steered the one-way *Oka* jet-propelled flying bomb-rockets. The torpedo-shaped, stub winged *Oka* rockets were called *Baka* by the Yanks. *Baka* means "idiot" in Japanese. They were flying bombs packed with nearly three thousand pounds of high explosives, carried under the belly of a medium or heavy bomber. Once near the target, they were released, to be ridden into the target by a suicide pilot who served as a living aim and exploder device.

Besides the plane and rocket pilots, there were other

139

death-dedicated suicide volunteers. Speedboats, packed with high explosives, were used, too. Midget submarines, operated by one or two suiciders, were used as living torpedoes. They actually were torpedoes fitted with housings in which Jap volunteers rode as living aim and firing mechanisms.

Before it was stopped, the grisly "Divine Wind" took a terrible toll. This last-gasp struggle alone killed over twelve thousand Americans, and wounded many times that number. On Okinawa itself nearly seven thousand GIs and Marines died. At sea it cost the U.S. Navy more men and ships than any other comparable battle-time campaign. Over five thousand seamen dead; another five thousand wounded; thirteen destroyers and one destroyer-escort sunk; thirteen carriers, ten battleships, and five cruisers severely damaged; and forty-seven destroyers and destroyer-escorts mauled and battered. How many Japs died, no one will ever know. This battle ended the Japanese empire.

The Picket Line at Okinawa was the worst ordeal ever faced by the American Navy. Most of the blows were taken by the swift "small boy" ships. Their eggshell hulls, built for speed, not for slugging, were ill-suited to such brutal, head-on smashes. Nevertheless, they won out, by sheer guts and gunfire. They choked the "Divine Wind" in the throats of their foes. No less than ninety-eight destroyers and fifty-two destroyer escorts fought in "the last battle" of the Japanese. Sixty-one of them were hit in the furious day and night battles.

*Operation Iceberg* was the code name of the American invasion plan for Okinawa. It aimed to seize the big island as the base for the final invasion of the Japanese home islands. As March 1945 ended, the Fifth Fleet headed for the China Sea—and Okinawa. April 1st— ironically named "Love Day" was the opening day.

Well aware of the ferocity of defense to be expected, wise old Admiral Nimitz sent a huge force to tackle the formidable task. The Japs surely would fight like cornered animals to defend their home grounds. Nearly fifteen hundred American ships, manned by over half a million men, sailed west to the far end of the Pacific to beard the tiger

140

in his lair. Over twelve hundred transport and supply ships, carrying 182,000 assault troops, aimed for Okinawa, with some three hundred fighting ships to protect them.

In the great anchorage area off the west coast of the long, narrow island, the vast transport fleet would have to sit for days and weeks. Such a huge assemblage of juicy targets would tempt the Japanese to wild attacks. If they could destroy the transports, they could isolate the invasion army, for leisurely butchery later.

Protection of the transport area would depend on a distant screen of swift fighting ships—the DD's and DE's. In a ring encircling the island, the destroyers and destroyed escorts would patrol, on constant radar picket duty. They would guard the vital convoy lanes, and flash warnings of aircraft or other enemies approaching the vulnerable transport area. More important, they were to stop the attackers with a wall of anti-aircraft fire—and with their ships and bodies, if need be.

Seventy miles out from the island coast the first picket line took stations. Forty miles from shore the second line began its picket runs. Then, twenty miles out from the transport area the last line was set up. The rings of picket groups were named *Task Flotilla 5*.

In each little picket group a fighter-director team kept in constant touch with some assigned fighter squadron. Two LCS's or other support craft went with each picket group. They were called "The Pallbearers," with typically salty navy humor.

At first only one destroyer was assigned to each picket group. But as days of furious attacks followed one another, more were added. Towards the end, in May, two or three DD's were in each group. Four to twelve planes were assigned on call solely as cover for each picket group. Destroyer escorts, not heavily enough armed for the outer line, served in the inner lines.

As many as nineteen picket groups ringed the island until shore radar stations could be set up. In each, two, three or four DD's and two to four LCS's cruised, each group usually in an Indian-fighting circle, for mutual

141

help. Whenever enemy planes were spotted, timely warning enabled the transport area guards to blanket the helpless transports with protective smoke.

It was up to the "tin cans." The big carriers, much too clumsy for this job, stood far away beyond the horizon. Their fighter planes came on call. Bombardment battleships and cruisers came in for short-time gun attacks on the island, and as quickly drew back from the danger zone. Blockading submarines stood far out, to warn of approaching surface attack.

It was from the air that danger would come. For that, the destroyermen were sent out. As usual, the men of the "tin can navy" went to it quickly, quietly, efficiently—and bravely.

*U.S.S. Hadley* joined one of the picket groups (group 15, north of the transport area), like all the other DD's, and settled down to alert patroling. It was not a new job to many of her men; but it was to some. She had been commissioned only a few months before. A fighter-director team was aboard, to control the twelve fighter planes assigned to this group's control.

*Hadley* was a good ship, with a good crew. One gun pointer of her crew, for example, was Jim Kaslov of Sharon, Pennsylvania. Kaslov once said: "After all, the ship is only a mount for the guns." He was right. His twin-40 crew could knock the eye off a mosquito at one thousand yards. And the crews of the five-inchers and other guns were just about as good. It was well for this ship's crewmen that they knew their business. Their lives were to depend on their skill—and intestinal fortitude.

*Hadley* worked in a team with another crack DD—the *Evans*. Between them, they were to blast some forty-five suicide planes and rockets out of the air in one terrific day. Incredible as it sounds, that score was literally true. One day of furious action—May 11th—was typical of how the iron men in the "tin ships" could fight.

Early in the morning of the 11th, the Kamikazes came like flies. Out of a misty haze to the north, the first one came, straight for *Hadley*.

Lookouts shrilled the alarm, and tense men at the guns

142

crouched ready. The tiny spot in the sky grew rapidly bigger. It was a float plane, the first of over 140 mad death-seekers that were to attack the two destroyers that day.

As the racing Kamikaze came into range the guns of the *Hadley* opened up with a snarling roar. Tracers and bursting shells began to spot the sky around the Jap plane. Suddenly there was a terrific explosion about fifteen hundred yards from the destroyer. The plane disappeared in a blasting flash of yellow flame and grey smoke. Direct hit—right on the nose! One Kamikaze gone to join his ancestors; first score for the *Hadley*.

Another plane came hurtling out of the mist, higher up this time. The gun muzzles on the destroyer rose swiftly, like insect feelers, pointing towards the new enemy. Behind the guns, tight-lipped crewmen braced for the next attack. Mount captains and gun captains spoke tersely to their crews. Ammunition and powder men swung to their jobs. Pointers peered through their sights.

While the guns lifted their muzzles, the fighter-director chief studied his radar screen and spoke to his air unit. "Bandits coming in from the north. We've got a snowstorm of Bogies, one five zero. Big raid coming up." Back on the carriers, far over the horizon, waiting fighter planes roared along flight decks, and leaped into the air. CAP (Combat Air Patrol) would be wanted—and how! The mist was swarming with Kamikazes.

The approaching plane was a Val. Snapping gunfire on the *Hadley* mounted to a roar, as the ship heeled around to bring all guns to bear. Fire control men sweated suddenly as the careening plane swerved and maneuvered, swinging around in an arc to hit from the rear. How could they figure the deflection rate? The plane swerved from side to side, skidding, slipping and barrel rolling; speeding up and slowing down, in a great circle.

At five thousand yards the air around the careening Val was plastered with 5-inch bursts, while streaming 40 mm. tracers seemed to frame the darting, dancing plane. Still it came on, closer and closer. At two thousand yards it turned sharply, and bored in toward the ship. The

143

20 mm. guns opened up, adding their shrill racket to the uproar. A thin wisp of black smoke began to stream from the on-rushing plane.

As it came on, right over the ship's wake, the after five-inchers crashed savagely. Each blast almost knocked down the crew of the nearby aft 20 mm. gun. Cold sweat beaded the gunners' brows.

The Val was smoking badly now, but it still came on like a rocket.

Yammering guns ripped desperately at the plunging Kamikaze, tearing at the wings and fuselage. Suddenly, a wing seemed to detach itself from the on-rushing plane. It floated like a leaf, swaying to and fro as it dropped. Then the plane turned lazily up into a long, graceful arch and flipped over on one side. Its dead pilot, riddled by flying steel, no longer controlled the explosive-packed machine. It dropped suddenly, nose first, and plunged into the sea, in a splashing column of foam—not a hundred yards from the *Hadley*.

As the guns suddenly fell silent, the men of the *Hadley* stared at each other, ashen-faced. How much of this sort of thing could men take? That plane had been death itself, plunging at them like a ghastly nightmare of murderous purpose. How long can men who want to live fight off men who want to die?

Veterans of dozens of deadly battles bit their lips, and clenched their fists to keep their hands from trembling. This wasn't battle. It was insanity—lunatic idiocy!

That was the reaction of all the men, in all the racing DD's and DE's of the great picket line. Each ship, in the whole long, scattered line was to go through this soul-searing experience—not just once, but many times. Off Okinawa, the seamen of America fought not only men, but grim, brain-addled death itself. That they stayed on, and fought this nightmare enemy to the end, almost passes belief.

But they stayed.

Here and there, on the crowded little ships, a man's nerves broke. A few men became hysterical, gibbering

144

with horror as the maniacs crashed into their ships. But the ones who cracked were very few. Almost every man held on and took it. Sick with horror and disgust, they stayed put, and beat off the swarming lunatics; and patched their ships after weird collisions with death-drunk foes, to fight again.

*Hadley* was only one of the many destroyers at Okinawa. Her men were only one crew, of the many who rode through the inferno there. They are symbols, one man for hundreds, one crew for many, one ship for all. In these sailors, American men-at-war reached an incredible peak of sheer cold courage, against insane enemies armed with horrible weapons and bent on death.

Over 140 suicide planes hurled themselves at the *Hadley* and the *Evans* alone on that awful day in May. Wave after wave of madmen came hurtling out of the sky. How many more were shot down, high above, in wild aerial dogfights, no one will ever know.

For almost two hours the waves of suicide planes came roaring at the defiant ship. One after another, they were beaten off. As the bellowing guns thudded and spat, their muzzles became black with powder flash. Gunners and crewmen became glassy-eyed with endless tension and effort. A few exhausted men retched and vomited with shock and nausea; but they came back to their posts, every time.

Each time, after the first solo attacks, four, five, or six Japs would plunge at the *Hadley* together. One would dive straight down from above. One would come screaming down at a 45° angle. Another would come gliding in at 30°. And another would skim the waves, low and level. From every quarter of the compass, they bored in on the racing destroyer—some bow-on, some from astern, and some from the sides.

Her guns spat death back at the plunging Kamikazes. Like a porcupine, her guns bristled in all directions, fighting off attackers. A canopy of streaming steel, flame, and smoke hung over her, like a wall to hold off the swarms above. Her men labored and sweated, feeding and firing their guns like lost souls doomed to everlasting labor in the fiery pits of hell.

By 0900 the *Evans* was three miles away, desperately fighting for her own life. Then *Evans* was hit, and out of action; and *Hadley* was alone under the buzzing beehive of maniacs.

From 0830 to 0900 the keen-eyed gunners on *Hadley* speared one plane after another—twelve in all. In a weltering chaos of diving planes and roaring guns firing in all directions, she splashed the sea with a dozen dead Jap planes.

At 0905 the weird attackers pierced her defenses. A high-flying Jap bomber released a *Baka*. Like a jet-propelled stone the huge rocket fell straight onto the *Hadley*. With a terrific explosion it tore through her deck, shattering power and control connections. A spout of flame boiled up from the stricken destroyer. Torn fragments of dead men littered her seared decks, as repair crews ran to stop her wounds. Burning and racked with pain, the little ship fought on. Then a hurtling bomb smashed into her, tearing at her vitals. Then a *Nate* plummeted onto the *Hadley,* crashing aft on the deck.

Shattering explosion tore the gallant ship, blowing her steadfast after gunners to shreds. But the other guns kept right on firing.

Another *Val* was driving for the hull of the stricken destroyer. Oblivious to the storm of flying steel, the fanatic Jap pilot held his "Divine Wind" plane straight in line to crash. It struck square amidships.

A dull, jarring boom signaled the smash. Terrific concussion drove in the side of the staggering ship. Water rushed in. Drunkenly, the *Hadley* began to heel over. Tons of green water pressed her down. She began to list and settle.

But the men on *Hadley* were still fighting. Every gun that had not been blasted was still firing.

The last of the howling Kamikazes came on, to finish the job. Clawing, spitting gunfire ripped it out of the sky, plunging it to its death in a foaming geyser in the sea. It was as though the furious men of the *Hadley* were reaching long, talon-tipped claws into the sky, tearing their tormentors down. Then suddenly, they were gone. There were no more left.

Wallowing heavily, Hadley seemed to be mortally wounded. Damage repair crews seemed to be losing the grim struggle with fire and water. At any moment she might roll over and sink.

Calm and restrained, the captain's voice sounded the order to prepare to abandon ship. But grief and pain racked him even as he gave the necessary order. Mullaney himself, and some forty officers and men, stayed aboard.

In quick, orderly fashion, life rafts were pushed over the side. The wounded were carried gently to safety on the rafts, and most of the crew went over the side too. Their LST's (the Pallbearers) were coming up fast, to lend a hand.

On board, the few remaining men labored in frantic haste, lightening the laboring ship and stopping her wounds. In a frenzied half-hour of homeric labor the damage was brought under control: Hadley would live, after all!

Battered, torn, and fiercely triumphant, Hadley did survive, after her unbelievable ordeal. Laboring heavily, she was towed to safety at Ie Shima, just southwest of Okinawa. She would ride the seas again. Her mission was accomplished. She had given the Japanese a bitter bellyful of suicide. And the transports she had protected were safe.

Hadley paid the price, as did so many other destroyers of the immortal "Picket Line." Twenty-eight of her men were dead. Sixty-seven were terribly wounded. The ship was a battered mess. But she was still there, and her indomitable men were triumphant.

The Kamikaze had blown itself out. What was the use of suicide tactics that cost almost twenty-five crack planes and pilots to damage one little ship! Not the grinning mask of death itself could break the American destroyermen. The Japanese were finished, and they knew it.

147

That was how it was on "the madhouse run" in the Okinawa picket line. It took iron men. Lucky for America that her destroyer sailors *are* iron men. Their flesh and bones can be torn and smashed, like other men's. But their will and courage are of hard, unbreaking stuff. They faced the ultimate enemy at Okinawa—gibbering death itself—and won.

It was a solemn roll call, when the battle was over. Many a fine ship and its men were gone forever—the *Abele,* the *Bush,* the *Callaghan,* the *Colhoun,* the *Drexler,* the *Little,* the *Longshaw,* the *Luce,* the *Morrison,* the *Oberrender,* the *Pringle,* the *Porter,* the *Twiggs,* the *Underhill.* And many DD's and DE's torn and battered, like *Hadley* and *Evans,* and the gallant *Hazelwood, Leutze, Hyman, Bennion,* and *Laffey,* to name only a few of the sixty-one that were scarred there.

What a fearful toll the little ships exacted from the Mikado's madmen can only be guessed. Suffice it to say that Japan was utterly broken and defeated when this battle ended. The United States Naval Institute *History of Destroyer Operations in World War II* hazards a guess, but says that it is only a guess.

All in all, it says, the Japs lost about 7,830 aircraft in the great defeat at Okinawa—over three thousand by Navy and Marine planes, and over 410 by Navy guns; two-thirds of these by guns of the DD's and DE's. A tremendous additional number were spotted and targeted by the destroyer fighter-director teams. They set up the enemy aircraft for the kill by American planes. Undoubtedly, the real score for the destroyers ran well into four figures.

Be that as it may, the important thing is this: destroyers are the bulk, sinews, and ranging power of the United States Navy. They are the workhorses of the ocean teams. Destroyermen are the real strength of our fighting ships, our wall of iron men.

At Okinawa, American destroyermen wrote in blood and fire a sage of courage and fighting hearts that will never die. Against the most fearful death-seeking foemen in history, they fought and won.

The United States Naval Institute, and many seamen who fought the Kamikaze, said of suicide-plane attacks that they were "practically impossible to stop."

But the destroyermen at Okinawa stopped them.

# I FOUGHT THE AMERICANS
# AT MIDWAY

### By Lt. Commander Sesu Mitoya
### Formerly of the Imperial Japanese Navy

WHEN first I heard of the planned attack on Midway, I was delighted. Like most Japanese naval officers in early 1942, I was sure of Japan's coming victory over the United States. This operation promised good opportunities to win glory for Dai Nippon, and perhaps a promotion.

I was communications officer on the proud aircraft carrier *Kaga*. Then a lieutenant commander, I served under the command of Captain Jisaku Okada. One of my best friends, Lt. Commander Tadashi Musumi, was commander of all the gun crews on board our big CV (aircraft carrier). It was one of the finest ships in the fleet—a happy ship with a fine, tightly knit complement of crewmen and airmen.

Early in April, planning for the invasion of Midway began. This was to be Japan's longest strike eastward, far across the Pacific, almost to the Hawaiian Islands. Its purpose was to seize a distant outpost, beyond which the American fleet could be held. This would cut off American communications with Australia. More important, it aimed to draw out the American fleet, and force it to give battle. We were sure that we could win that battle. How mistaken we were, I know now.

Our operation plan was gigantic. My group, the First Carrier Striking Force, led by Vice Admiral Chuichi Nagumo, was to strike from the northwest, at Midway. Not far south of us, striking straight out of the west, was the main Battleship Force, led by the revered Admiral Isoroku Yamamoto himself. Further south, and coming in from the southwest, was the Transport-Invasion group, led by Vice Admiral Nobutake Kondo, with a Close Support Group led by Vice Admiral Kurita.

Two diversionary groups led by Vice Admiral Hosogaya were to invade the Aleutian Islands, far to the north, at the same time. They were to seize Adak, Kiska, and Attu Islands there. At least they were successful—for a while. M-Day was set for June 7th.

After the war ended, we learned that the Americans knew all about our plans. By an incredible feat of military intelligence, they had broken our code. Every message radioed from Tokyo or from our ships was perfectly understood by the Americans. They were waiting for us— had we only known it. American naval, air and ground forces were concentrating at Midway.

Late in May, all our task forces sortied from their bases, and headed east, to the attack. En route, we picked up a code message sent by an American submarine, apparently warning Midway of our approach.

In our Carrier Striking Force, we were not a bit concerned about it. We could not decode the message. But we nonchalantly reasoned that it served our purpose. After all, we wanted the Americans to come out and fight. We had the foolish vanity of self-delusion.

My group was so powerful that we feared nothing. In it were carriers *Akagi, Kaga* (my vessel), *Hiryu,* and *Soryu,* the mightiest aircraft carriers afloat. With us were battleships *Haruna* and *Kirishima,* plus cruisers *Chickuma, Tone,* and *Nagara,* eleven destroyers, and several submarines. Not far away, in Admiral Yamamoto's force, were battleships *Yamato, Mutsu,* and *Nagato,* light carrier *Hosho,* cruiser *Sendai,* seaplane carriers *Chiyoda* and *Nishin,* and nine more destroyers. We outnumbered any possible American fleet then known to be in the Pacific.

In fact, we later learned that the American forces at Midway consisted of about 2000 infantry ashore, plus carriers *Hornet, Enterprise* and *Yorktown,* with seven or eight cruisers, thirteen or fourteen destroyers, and a few submarines. This task force waited to the northeast of our invasion track, ready to hit us on the flank.

Late in the day, on June 4th, as we neared Midway, we received reports of air attacks on the southern transport group. Our high optimism began to fade. It was clear that the enemy knew of our approach. Nevertheless, we steamed on.

Far to the north, the Aleutians attack force was having its troubles, too. Our fliers and planes were not well prepared for the cold and fog there. Their engines were failing, and little damage was done by bombing in thick fog.

All the signs were ominous. But we were so drunk on victories in the opening battles of the war, that we sadly misjudged the danger. The next day, we were in the attack zone.

Before dawn on June 5th, from over 200 miles northwest of Midway, our first air attack wave was launched from Admiral Nagumo's carriers. Excitement was in the air, aboard the *Kaga*.

Loudspeakers barked: "Aviators assemble for the strike!" And soon after, "Launching stations, ready? Start engines!" Shattering uproar bellowed on the flight deck, and livid streaks of engine exhausts flamed in the darkness.

Launching lights illuminated the deck. "Commence launching!" sounded from the bridge. The air officer swung his green signal lamp in a circle. One by one our Zero fighters roared forward, and leaped into the air. Cheers of crewmen echoed above the engines' roars. Then the dive bombers followed. Soon over 100 planes, from all the carriers, were in the air. Then the second wave planes moved into positions for launching.

Somehow, I was worried, despite the general excitement. We were dangerously near Midway, and with hardly more than a dozen planes left to guard the carrier force.

Fully alerted American defense planes met our planes over the Midway islands. A fierce air battle exploded as our dive bombers dove in to hit installations on Sand Island and Eastern Island. We lost four bombers and two fighters, while little effective bomb damage was done. Our second wave results were much the same.

On board *Kaga,* about 0500, the alarm bugle suddenly sounded "Air raid!" Our remaining fighters quickly raced out to intercept. Reports flashed through my Communications Center, confused and uncertain. Enemy planes here, there, all about us. But we could see none.

At 0700 we saw them for the first time. Six came from one side, four from the other. They looked like torpedo planes. Our fighters wheeled to meet them. Our cruisers and destroyers opened up with racketing anti-aircraft fire.

Black bursts of explosions dotted the sky all around the on-rushing American planes. Still they came on, hardly above the sea's surface. Our Zeros dove through our own anti-aircraft fire, guns blazing at the Americans. One by one, three of the torpedo planes spouted flame and smoke, and then crashed into the sea.

The others kept bravely on. Then they released their torpedoes. As the planes swung away we could plainly see their white star markings. They were B-26's. Only three got away. Not one torpedo hit its target as our ships turned and maneuvered to avoid them.

At 0850 our own planes returned. With furious speed out carrier crews labored to re-arm them. While this went on, I received word from Admiral Kondo's force that an enemy force of a carrier and cruisers and destroyers was approaching. We turned to meet it.

At 0930 we launched planes again. Fifty Zeros sped to meet another American force of fifteen torpedo bombers. We were too many for them. None of the American planes got through to our carriers. We watched one speck after another, high in the sky, spark into flame and plummet down, trailing black smoke.

On board, our men cheered and whistled wildly as our planes scored. Then another group of six planes came n at us, charging in again and again through the anti-aircraft fire. The Americans were brave. Torpedoes streaked the water. But luck was with us. None struck.

Zero after Zero exhausted its ammunition, and returned to our decks to re-arm. While service crews cheered our pilots, the planes were hastily re-armed and launched again and again. At 1020 it happened that most of our planes were on deck, readying to take off again. Bombs were carelessly stacked in piles near the planes. We seemed to be winning steadily.

Suddenly a lookout yelled "Dive bombers!" I looked up. Five black, fat-bellied planes were hurtling down at us. I recognized them at once—American Hell Divers.

As I looked, tiny black specks detached themselves from the planes. The specks grew larger. Bombs, coming right down on us!

I was standing on the flight deck, near the tower. Quickly I dove flat to the deck. The horrible scream of the dive bombers rose to a shriek. Then a crashing roar shook the *Kaga*. A bright flash glared, through the sleeve I held over my eyes. Then another blast—and another.

A gush of hot air washed over me. We were hit—hard! The barking of anti-aircraft guns began to be mixed with a rushing, roaring sound. We were afire!

I leaped to my feet. Horrified, I saw gaping holes in the flight deck, near the amidship elevator. The elevator was a twisted mass of metal, half drooped into the hangar. The deck plates were a crazy jumble of torn metal.

On deck, many planes were overturned, in flames. Some stood tilted on their wings, tails up. Orange flame and black smoke boiled up through them, belching out of their tails like chimneys.

I could see, not far off, the *Akagi* and the *Soryu*. They too were aflame, with black smoke rolling from their decks. It seemed unbelievable. In seconds our invincible carrier force had become shattered wrecks. Tears welled to my eyes. It was a terrible scene.

On deck, and in the Ready Room, burned and mangled men writhed and groaned. Deep in the big carrier's vitals rending explosions shook her. As fire spread, the heaps of bombs and torpedoes began to explode, with shattering blasts. Spraying steel fragments ripped the bridge. The *Kaga* was an inferno, with scorched, blackened men staggering about in helpless confusion.

The fire control officer, Lieutenant Fiyuma, came to

the bridge. There I was awaiting orders, near Captain Okado. The captain stood and stared, half-dazed, like a man in a dream.

Fiyuma reported that all passages below were afire. Most of the crew were trapped, burning inside the ship. We had to go to the anchor deck quickly, if we wished to escape. The carrier was beginning to list ominously.

Crewmen were laboring valiantly to try to stop the enormous fires—in vain. All power was off. Many men were torn to pieces by the repeated explosions. Surgeons worked like automatons on endless lines of torn bodies. As fire-laden air erupted from the ship, many men collapsed with suffocation.

I spoke to Captain Okada, trying to rouse him from his stupefied reverie. It was now near midday. Our escort destroyers, *Hagikas* and *Makaze,* could take off survivors. Unless we abandoned ship soon she would take us all down with her.

The captain shook his head vaguely. "I will remain with my ship," he said. More planes were coming in. I went to the Ready Room, to try again to contact the men below in the Engine Rooms.

While I was below, other bombers struck the *Kaga.* Where they came from, I do not know. When I rushed back to the bridge—there was no bridge. A direct hit had smashed the ship's nerve center. Captain Okada and Fiyuma were dead. My good friend Musumi was dead, too. Commander Amagay, the air officer, as senior-surviving officer, had assumed command.

About an hour later the *Kaga* was a blackened hulk, half-tilted over. Then, to add to our misery, someone shouted "Torpedo!" A submarine had loosed a torpedo at us.

Holding my breath, I prayed as the deadly tin fish came at us, leaving a white wake behind as it approached. It struck. But by some miracle it did not explode. A dud! It broke in half. Some of our men, swimming nearby, after being blown overboard, swam to the floating section of the torpedo. Ironically, the deadly weapon served them as a life raft.

155

Finally, at 1600, Commander Amagay ordered "Abandon ship!" We began to send men down ropes to our waiting destroyers. The *Kaga* was a vast funeral pyre. Over 800 men, nearly one-third of her crew, were dead.

We watched with tears in our eyes as our proud *Kaga* settled deeper and deeper. Boiling smoke and pillars of fire shrouded our beloved ship. At 1800 she seemed to leap in the water as two terrific explosions shook her. Then, still stately in death, she sank forever beneath the waves.

Not far away, *Soryu* and *Akagi* went down, too, with black pillars of smoke marking their graves. We turned to follow *Hiryu,* the only carrier left of our great Striking Force. It was June 6th, a fateful day for Nippon.

Planes from the last carrier reported dire news. The American fleet was closing in for the kill. In it were no less than three carriers—*Hornet, Enterprise,* and *Yorktown.*

Huddled aboard the crowded destroyer *Hagikaze,* we looked at each other in silent wonder. But Admiral Yamaguchi, on the *Hiryu,* chose to go on fighting. The *Hiryu's* planes rose to launch another attack. Weak and exhausted as we were, we survivors of *Kaga* cheered as the Zeros zoomed over us, bound to engage the enemy.

An hour later the planes returned—half of them. They had hit the *Yorktown.* But while they were gone the sky was full of American planes, attacking the *Hiryu* and our destroyers. Surely a hundred planes attacked the last of our carriers.

At 1700, torpedo bombers, hidden in the glare of the setting sun, got through the curtain of anti-aircraft fire of all our ships. Thirteen planes hit the gallant *Hiryu.* Others hit the battleship *Haruna* and cruiser *Tone.* As darkness fell, *Hiryu* was a blazing hulk. Her last planes had no haven when they returned. We were defeated, indeed.

So, as night mercifully hid us, our shattered fleet turned for home. The *Hiryu* was scuttled by torpedoes from our own destroyers. The long, harried retreat west began.

But we were not yet finished. At dawn, as American planes hovered on the horizon, we turned for a last blow at our invisible pursuers. We had only a few spotter planes and two light carriers to see for us. Of radar we knew nothing.

The rest is history, too. In a wild series of running battles, the next day, both sides lost more ships. One of our submarines sank the carrier *Yorktown* and destroyer *Hamman*. Our cruisers *Mogami* and *Mikuma* and destroyer *Arasho* were crippled. We were harried and driven west, towards home and safety. Fortunately, foul weather hid our withdrawal.

On June 7th all contact with the enemy was broken. Hidden by fog and foul weather, our battered fleet limped for home.

So ended the dream of Japanese empire. The only small prizes we had won were two rocky islands in the Aleutians, Attu and Kiska, neither of which we would be able to hold. The peak of Japanese power had been reached, and passed. From this point forward the road of Nippon was ever downward, into the depths of slow, sure, and bitter defeat.

The catastrophe at Midway had been the turning of the tide—and deep in our hearts, we Japanese knew it. Thenceforth the fatal tide of war drove us inevitably on to final calamity and to the soul-tearing sorrow of capitulation.

It has been said that Midway was an American victory of intelligence. That is true. Not only did the Americans know our every move, but we dismally failed to locate the enemy forces. So it happened that a smaller American fleet destroyed our scattered groups piecemeal, one by one.

In truth, our worst error was caused by our vanity. We underestimated our adversaries, to our chagrin and pain. This was unforgivable, when we well knew the bravery, skill, and boldness of the Americans. We were blind with conceit and overweening confidence. Even so, had we had the secrecy and surprise we imagined, the outcome might have been different.

The final accounting, after the battle, told the full

157

story of our defeat. We had lost four major aircraft carriers—*Kaga, Akagi, Soryu,* and *Hiryu,* and two cruisers—*Mikuma* and *Mogami*; plus damage to destroyers *Asashio* and *Arashio,* destroyer escort *Tanikaze,* transport *Haruna,* and oiler *Akebono Maru*; as well as about 325 planes and thousands of men.

The Americans had lost the carrier *Yorktown* and destroyer *Hamman,* plus over 140 planes. Compared to the loss of our four carriers, the backbone of the Japanese fleet, the American losses were small.

As for me, I was in the depths of despair as we plodded west. Never again was I to sail aboard a carrier. Staff and command officers who lose their ships do not get promotions. I was to spend the rest of the war at dull, stupid paperwork, ashore. For me, the days of battle glory were over for good.

But at least I can say this: When Japan fought the epic battle of Midway, in the bright noon of her glory, I was there, serving the Mikado and Dai Nippon.

# THE DIEPPE RAID:
# AN EPIC OF CANADIAN COURAGE

### By Furman Keith III

CANADIANS DO NOT go in much for boasting. Probably that is why today, the great Dieppe Raid is nearly forgotten, while many lesser amphibious battles are well remembered.

But the Dieppe landing of World War II was the model for all the seaborne invasions, since. And the quiet Canadians, gentle and modest in time of peace, showed again how terrific they can be in time of war. They formed the core of the assault force, in which also were Britons, Scots, Americans, Frenchmen, and indeed representatives of all the Allied World.

The typical Canadian attitude towards boasting, was summed up by one sergeant's remark to a recruit, who sounded off about how tough he'd be. Said the sergeant: "Not so much bloody mouth! Let's *see* what you do, not hear about it!"

Backbone of the almost recklessly daring raid, was the Canadian 2nd Division, spearheaded by the Royal Regiment of Canada, plus the Royal Hamilton Light Infantry, the Canadian Essex Scottish, the South Saskatchewan Regiment, the Cameron Highlanders of Canada, the Fusiliers Mont Royal, and the 14th Canadian Army Tank Battalion with the Calgary Regiment.

An inter-Allied Commando unit was formed to aid the predominantly Canadian task force. It included British and Free French Commandos and American Rangers. British, American, and Allied air units, and British naval units aided by a few American ships would support the assault. They, too, would execute and cover the withdrawal after the raiding attack was over.

The great attack had two prime purposes. One was to test the German defenses of *Festung* (Fortress) *Europa,* to take prisoners, and bring back military papers and information. More important, it would put to the acid test of battle all the Anglo-American theories and plans for the final invasion, that would liberate Europe from German slavery. It would provide a basis of bloody experience for the enormous Normandy invasion as well as for many other landings in the Mediterranean and in the Pacific.

On August 19th, 1942, the day of the raid, the Nazi juggernaut was at the peak of its power. Small Commando raids had been made at Vaagso, Lofoten, St. Nazaire, and Boulogne. But this was to be the first large scale assault landing against a heavily defended coast. It was to be the Allies' first real challenge to the "invincible" German stronghold, and their first large-scale killing of Boche in that stronghold.

The French seacoast town of Dieppe is just sixty-four miles south of the English coast town of Eastbourne, across the stormy English Channel. Dieppe is a resort town, flanked by other similar seaside towns—Varengeville and Pourville to the west towards Havre, and Berneval to the east near where the coast turns north to Boulogne and Calais.

Rough, quiet Canadians, silent-moving in rubber soled boots, assembled quietly for the fateful raid. Combined Operations HQ, under the then Vice Admiral Lord Louis Mountbatten, had planned the myriad details of the operation, working with General McNaughton, Canadian Commander in Britain. Second Division's CO, Major General J. H. Roberts, would lead the actual attack.

The plan was simple in design, but complex in execution. Commandos were to land first, to silence big coastal batteries flanking Dieppe. The Royal Regiment of Canada would go in at Puits, and the South Saskatchewans at Pourville. Behind would come the Cameron Highlanders of Canada.

160

On the main Dieppe beaches would land the Canadian Essex Scottish, the Fusiliers Mount Royal, the Royal Hamilton Light Infantry, and the 14th Canadian Army Tank Battalion. American Rangers would accompany each unit in the pre-dawn assault, to gain experience for later American landing operations. Pre-landing sea and air bombardment and protective fire to cover the withdrawal, were planned in intricate detail.

Aboard the ships plowing slowly across the channel, the men made themselves as comfortable as they could. Games of cards passed the tense, dragging minutes. Poker and "liar" games for small stakes helped to take men's minds off the coming ordeal. Others just sat quietly and waited.

Said Corporal Peter McDonald of Toronto to Private George Smith of Collingwood: "Every man of the Royals will damn well know more about the map of Dieppe than about his own home town!"

Smith grinned briefly. "Nobody would sleep through map-reading drill if a Nazi gun was waiting as the final test! The goddam Huns know the place well. We'd best know it too!"

One group of soldiers, gathered in a foc'sl, spent the time singing ribald songs—"Round Her Knee She Wore a Purple Garter," and other bawdy soldier songs.

Then, in shadowy darkness, "Action stations" sounded, and the men filed quietly to their assigned posts. One trooper's remark in the tense darkness spoke for all. "It's a good thing the other bastards are more scared than we are!"


The men crowded silently into the square-bowed landing craft. Gunners around the Bren gun braced on a starboard thwart, crouched near their weapon. Through the shadows flashes and dull booms on the distant shore told of the preliminary air bombardment. The boats wallowed uncertainly for a minute on the choppy water, then turned and moved towards the open beaches.

On the far left flank, near Berneval, terrible luck struck the Commando unit boats there. By pure chance a German convoy happened to be passing by, hugging the shore.

161

It was escorted by four heavily armed flak ships and several E-Boats.

Smashing fire from the flak ships tore the boats of the Commandos, wreaking horrible damage. This was a freak break for the Germans that no one could have predicted. The invading craft ran smack into the passing gunboats. Almost all the landing craft were sunk, and many helpless men burdened with arms and ammunition sank to death in the bullet and shell torn waters. Only one landing boat got to the shore.

Worse still, the uproar of gunfire near Berneval echoed down the other beaches. Forewarned, German troops rushed to their defense posts at most of the other beaches.

*Even so, the twenty men of the one boat at Berneval attacked their task force's target, in a breath-taking display of bravery. For four hours they dueled with the 200 Germans and big guns of the Berneval battery, inflicting great damage. Then they boldly re-embarked and withdrew, their mission accomplished.*

Many men would have turned and fled at such a sickening turn of luck. Not the Canadians! Grim and pale-faced even under their black-cork-smudged camouflage, they came on against the alerted defenses.

Ramps crashed down and men streamed towards the few gullies and trails leading up from the beaches. Parties of Pioneer unit men pushed long pipes of Bangalore torpedoes under coils of barbed wire. Cracking explosions blasted lanes through the defenses. Panting troopers dashed through, and began to climb the cliffs and spread into the fields.

In their fortified howitzer positions the German gunners began to fire at the ships lying offshore. In reply the ships' big guns began to spit back. The supporting naval bombardment of Dieppe began, while the ground troops worked their way towards the town. Thunderous sound boomed and echoed across the cliffs and beaches.

Overhead, flights of cannon-firing Hurricanes darted at the cliff tops, stabbing at the gun casemates and machine gun pits. Higher up, lumbering Boston bombers spilled clusters of black bombs down on the fortifications. Running men yelled up at the heedless planes: "Give 'em hell! Blast the bastards!"

Out of the east, swarms of Nazi planes came racing to challenge the invaders. Messerschmitts, Focke-Wulf 190's, Dorniers, Junkers, and Heinkels, and Spitfires tangled in a swarming, howling melee of dog-fights. Quite unexpectedly, the raid had stung the Luftwaffe into full scale action. It was to cost the Luftwaffe dear in lost planes and pilots.

On the cliff tops and in the fields just beyond, many savage little duels blazed briefly as the Canadians, Commandos, and Rangers closed in on gun positions. Many a little epic fight took place that morning, with bullets, grenades, and bayonets.

One trooper, Private Donald Furness, killed six Germans with one burst from his tommy gun. Another man, Troop Sergeant Major Stockdale of a Commando unit, had his foot blown away by a stick bomb, but kept on firing his gun as he lay terribly wounded. It was routine for men bleeding with serious wounds to go right on fighting.

Private Ralph Prentice, firing a mortar, was hit in the stomach by a sniper's bullet. He stayed at his weapon and kept firing. One of his shells struck a German ammo dump and blew it up with a roar that rocked the earth.

Private Joseph Spero, struck in the face and half blinded by a shell fragment, charged a machine-gun pit with his bayonet and killed three Germans with the cold steel.

All over the beaches and fields lay the huddled figures of dead and wounded men. Blood-soaked Canadians, their eyes rolling with agony, tried to crawl forward to help their mates. That was how it was with the Canadians. Sweating with the normal human fear of death and of howling, tearing steel, they yet pushed forward. Bravery was taken for granted.

The Berneval battery, four and a half miles east of Dieppe, alerted by the chance action of the flak ships, did real damage to the naval force. It sank one destroyer and a number of landing craft. But it was kept busy by the few men who had reached shore. Otherwise it would have raised havoc with the exposed ships below it.

Near Puits, E-Boats attacked the Royals' boats. Destroyer fire drove off the E-Boats. But the guns ashore took a heavy toll of the charging Royals. The first wave was almost annihilated.

Captain J. C. H. Anderson, his head bleeding from shell wounds, kept firing a Bren gun from his boat. Follow-up waves of the Royals pushed doggedly up the beach while men fell like wheat cut by a scythe. Taking terrible losses, they stubbornly kept on, until they had taken their objective.

At Pourville, the South Saskatchewans achieved complete surprise and stormed ashore almost unopposed. They were through the wire before the startled German defenders opened fire. Then enemy mortar and shell fire pounded them as their advance spearheads drove into the town itself. Dueling with the defenders, they opened the way for the Camerons of Canada to pass through and head for Dieppe as planned.

Lance Corporal Guy Berthelot typified the boldness of the South Saskatchewans. He took command of a platoon when all its officers and non-coms were lost. Then led it in a charge, guns firing from the hip as they ran, to kill twenty-nine Germans and capture a crucial hilltop.

The Camerons drove through, in a running fight two miles inland, killing Germans all along the way. Then they blasted their way out. Eighty percent of the Camerons fought their way back, many of them wounded.

For four hours the raiders shot and smashed their way through the thick defenses. Meanwhile, Royal Canadian Engineers led the assault at Dieppe itself. Then foot troops accompanied the Calgary Regiment's Churchill tanks in the assault right into the town.

There the Canadian Essex Scottish, Royal Hamilton Light Infantry, and French Canadian Fusiliers Mont Royal smashed into the fortress town. Guns in pillboxes, hotel windows, the Casino, and the Promenade smashed at their faces.

Through swirling smoke screens the Canadians drove forward against blazing volleys of fire. Tanks stopped on the beach or in streets kept firing as steel pillboxes. Cracking grenade and gunfire made a shambles, with dead and dying invaders and defenders scattered all through the burning town.

Raiders set fire to boats and barges with streams of bullets fired into oil tanks. Others destroyed the radio station and command posts. All the while they snatched military papers and maps, and herded terrified German prisoners back to the beach.

Typical of the fierce raiders was Lance Sergeant George Hickson of the Engineers. He led a platoon when the officers and non-coms were all killed or wounded, and stormed the Casino, the core fortress.

With dynamite charges he blasted through the walls. One of his charges blew in a steel door of a gun emplacement, killing the six-man gun crew. Then he blew up the six-inch gun and several machine gun nests.

The Fusiliers Mont Royal and Essex Scottish took heavy losses and inflicted worse on their enemies. It would take volumes to describe the dozens of acts of breathtaking courage and boldness of many men on that day of thundering battle.

But after four hours of shocking, brutal assault, all units of the raiders turned back, as ordered. Their mission accomplished, they each had to fight a way back, against swarming enemy reinforcements.

Drawn, exhausted men, fighting every step of the way, moved back to the beaches and re-embarked under ceaseless fire. They brought dead and wounded back with them, as best they could.

Once and for all they had punctured the myth of Hitler's *Festung Europa*. Despite all the Teutonic boasting, they had proved that the Nazi defenses could be pierced. They had put the fear of death and retribution into the hearts of the swaggering, brutal German "overlords."

It had cost much—2350 killed, wounded, and missing of the 5000 Canadians. Almost half of the raiding force were casualties, with the Canadians bearing the brunt.

Yet the great raid was a success. It was a "reconnaissance in force" that would insure the success of the

165

final invasion—*Operation Overlord* in Normandy. There, too, the Canadians would storm ashore, this time to stay, together with their British and American comrades.

Lance Sergeant Pierce Sondstrom of the Royals summed up the feelings of all the Canadians, as the battered survivors rocked homeward bound across the channel.

"Bloody rough, it was," he said. "But we showed them what's what—and what's coming to them!"

And ashore, the stunned Germans felt uncertainty rising thickly in them. If they had been unable to destroy this raid, what would happen when the full might of the British, Canadians, and Americans were unleashed against them?

What happened then, all the world knows. The free men of the western world utterly destroyed the evil Third Reich.

The Canadians at Dieppe had showed them how.

# BRIDGE OF DEATH

### By David Jacobson

I WAS SITTING at the bar, sipping beer. Larry, my favorite bartender on Cherokee Strip, had set one up on the house. Half way through my free one I heard this guy popping off again, telling how rough he had it in the damned army; the stupid drill sergeants, the ninety day wonders who rated a salute, and last, but by no means least, was the vituperation he spewed on the henhouse MP's. The outfit who were always behind the front lines, way behind.

And never saw combat.

I had heard this character sounding off before, as we sat next to each other bending elbows. I used to condescend, and say, when he got going on the war and the damned army, "There's always somebody that's a no good bastard in the army." And his stock reply was always, "And for my money it was the goddamn MP's. Bar none."

It was a hot August afternoon, and I wasn't in a particularly benevolent or tolerant mood. On the other hand, I wasn't trying to defend all MP's. I know what some of them are like. I was an MP some years ago, in Manila and Shanghai, with the 31st Infantry Regiment. I was fed up with his vilification of men who wore the blue and white brassard on their arms, and I was irked by some of his false and ignorant statements, which, if nothing else, proved one thing, he had never seen any action.

I proceeded to straighten him out, selecting the bloody episode at Remagen. And suddenly he ran out of descriptive adjectives. It stopped him cold.

It was three o'clock, on the afternoon of March 7, 1945,

167

when General Omar Bradley telephoned the Supreme Allied Commander, General Eisenhower, at Rheims. When Ike was informed that the Remagen bridge had been captured, he was elated. The capture of the strategic bridge changed the course of military action in Europe. And by nightfall, Remagen had become the focal point of action, in what proved to be the biggest break since D-Day, 6th of June, 1944.

The glory of capturing the bridge went to advance elements of the 1st battalion, 310 Infantry, 78th Division, attached to the 9th Armored division. Storming the two bridge towers, they killed or captured the German machine-gunners left behind by the Krauts, fleeing to the east bank of the Rhine.

All along the great river, the once invincible Nazi army was falling back in frantic confusion, blowing up bridges all along the Rhine, in their wake, trying to stem the Yank juggernaut. But someone, to use the army vernacular, had fouled up at Remagen, and the breech was made.

When Adolf Hitler was informed of the debacle at Remagen, he was furious. He sent for his Chief of Staff, Field Marshal von Runstedt. The Marshal's excuse made no difference. There was no acceptable excuse with the Fuehrer. In a fit of uncontrollable anger, he ripped the decorations from von Runstedt's uniform.

Five subordinate officers, directly responsible for the conduct of the war in the area, were executed for dereliction of duty in failing to destroy the bridge.

Not since Napoleon's forces swept across the Rhine at Ulm, more than a century ago, in 1805, had the historic Rhine been spanned by a foe. It proved to be the turning point of the war in Europe. But the hard-pressed Germans dug in east of Flak Hill, retaliating at long range, laying siege, a siege unparalleled for the area involved. A siege that took a staggering toll in American casualties.

It was 1900 hours, March 7, 1945, when Major Claire Thurston, provost marshal of the 9th Infantry Division, reported to General Craig for instruction. The division commander ordered Thurston to move his men out ahead

168

of the division, mark the route for the 47th Regimental Combat Team, the first large force scheduled to cross at dawn the next morning.

"I'll never forget that night," said Major Thurston. "It was a cold March night, and all along the winding road we were harassed by snipers, who tried to ambush our men— the mined road. It was an extremely difficult task. We arrived at the bridge around midnight."

By mutual arrangement with the 9th Armored Division provost marshal, Captain John Hyde, and his platoon took over the western approach to the bridge. Thurston and his company of 200 MP's worked the eastern approach and the entire length of the bridge.

Shortly before dawn, March 8, 1945, the 47th Regimental Combat Team, 78th Division, attached to the 9th Armored, began their historic march across the bridge.

Said Thurston: "Apparently German artillery spotters knew when there was any troop movement on the bridge, because the moment they set foot on the bridge, the Nazis on the other side of Flak Hill cut loose with everything they had.

"It was the most terrific sustained assault I've seen since D-Day. The mere crossing of the bridge was a hair-raising experience. The moment a man set foot on the bridge, it became a battle for survival. Many never reached the other side. The troops had to keep moving across the bridge of death, but my boys had to stay there."

Corporal Bruce Moyer, a young non-com from Detroit, was splicing a communication cable when there was a direct hit on the bridge by German artillery.

He stood there, spraddled legged, an amazed look on his grimy face. He looked down at his hands and saw he had only a three-foot stub of wire left.

"Goddamn," he cried, "those bastards can really call their shots."

But instead of running for cover, he resumed his task, completing his assignment.

Said Thurston, who witnessed the incident, "He was one of the bravest men I've ever seen."

169

Some of the soldiers had not been under such intense fire as they encountered when they began running the 1204-foot gauntlet of death. Some would freeze at the wheel, some panicked and jumped out, seeking refuge under jeeps and six by six's. Thurston's MP's would urge them on. When a convoy driver was hit, an MP would take over and finish the trip, and then return to his post on the bridge.

The German high command ordered the bridge destroyed at all cost, as the siege went on unabated. Suicidal attempts were made by the Luftwaffe pilots as they came sweeping from the east side of Flak Hill. The 82nd Anti-Aircraft downed four of the first attackers from the air. P-38's engaged reckless-flying Messerschmitts and low-flying Stukas, shooting down twenty-six enemy aircraft. And the dead game Yanks kept pouring across the bridge.

The desperation tactics of the enemy enabled them to make an occasional hit, and as Major Thurston put it, "It would vibrate like a banjo string, and I thought it was surely going down. But it didn't."

Every five minutes depth charges were dropped into the river and detonated to keep frog men and subs from getting under the bridge. High-powered lights played across the murky Rhine, constantly on the alert for floating objects.

Underwater demolition swimmers, trained by Count Skorzeny, who gained fleeting fame when he attempted to infiltrate our lines with English-speaking saboteurs, came down the river, towing high explosives in fabric bags. Equipped with oxygen tanks, they could stay under water for an hour. But doughboys and MP's on the bridge, with the aid of powerful searchlights, spotted them. And those who weren't shot or drowned, were driven ashore and captured.

Major Thurston, who made as many as thirty trips a day across the hotly contested bridge, had to seek replacements after the third day. General Craig authorized him to select twenty-five men from each regiment of the 9th Infantry Division. These doughboys donned MP brassards during battle.

170

This tunnel was also the collecting point for POW's. When approximately one hundred prisoners had been taken, they were run across the bridge to the west side.

Said Thurston: "There was no prodding the Germans when they set foot on that bridge. They ran so fast the MP's could hardly keep up with them.

MP Private Irving Hughes, of Hyattville, Maryland, was working the west end of the bridge. Time and again he had gone out and brought in wounded. One evening he saw four engineers hit by a shell. Hughes was near the point of exhaustion. He looked around, asking for volunteers. But there were no takers. Wearily he climbed into the jeep and went out by himself and brought the wounded men in.

PFC Albert Steadman was decorated for his part on the Remagen bridge. But like Sergeant Daniels and ten others of his company, the award was posthumous.

On the 17th of March, two pontoon bridges were put in service. The bridge had been turned over to the engineers for repairs. Major Thurston was sitting in his jeep on Flak Hill, when his orderly suddenly shouted, "Look, Major, the bridge is falling."

The provo turned his head in time to see the battered structure settling into the Rhine, pulling eight of the engineers with it into the icy waters, drowning them.

For ten days the bridge had withstood everything the Germans could throw at it. Ten days of literal hell for the 1st, 9th, and 99th Divisions who crossed it. As many as seven tank destroyers with a column of infantry on each side of the catwalk crossed the bridge at one time. Yet on the 17, with no troop movement or heavy equipment, and only three hundred engineers working on it, the bridge collapsed without any warning. The west end fell in first, pulling the east end loose from its mooring.

The saga of the bridge at Remagen had reached a bloody climax.

Ten of Thurston's MP's were cited for outstanding bravery.

"The Military Police Platoon, 9th Infantry Division, is cited for extraordinary gallantry and outstanding performance on the Ludendorff bridge at Remagen—

braving constant heavy artillery fire and air attacks every hour of the day—on two occasions V-2 weapons—unable to take cover, the MP's kept the vital artery clear—with no concern for personal safety, these men maintained control of the bridge with a magnificent display of courage and devotion to duty—"

This is a portion of what the Presidential Citation read, the first such award to MP's in their history. But perhaps the best summary of that history-making epic, is what some of the men who crossed the bridge at Remagen had to say.

Fighting men who remembered MP's like Steadman, Hughes, Moyer, Hatfield, Kretchmar, Nute, Daniels, and many others. MP's armed with burp guns, rifles, hand grenades and .45's. Combat MP's.

Invariably when they spoke to Thurston about the never-to-be-forgotten Remagen incident, they'd say, "Major, I know how scared I was, just crossing that bridge. And just think, those guys had to stay there, hour after hour, night and day, with no foxholes to hide in.

"They sure had a helluva lot of guts."

# HE BUILT A BETTER MOUSETRAP

### By Dale Varney

THE TRAP had been prepared months before. The idea for the massive German counteroffensive in the Ardennes was first broached during the summer of 1944.

"The Great Blow," was how the Nazi high command referred to the operation during its planning stages.

"The counteroffensive will be the great blow against the Allies," Hitler told his generals. "The assault will drive the Americans and English back to the sea . . ."

Gerd von Rundstedt was the man who would serve as the genius of the "Great Blow." A German general of the old school, a monacled, aristocratic Junker, von Rundstedt was an ideal choice for the task.

War was his sole interest—his entire life. He was one of those whose entire career was concerned exclusively with military matters. Gerd von Rundstedt considered warfare a cold, exact science. He could be relied upon to plan the huge campaign down to the last and tiniest detail.

There were other reasons why he was chosen. Main among these was the fact that he was popular with officers and men of the battered Wehrmacht. The grim-visaged, ramrod-straight general had earned and maintained the respect not only of the "regulars," but even of the SS troops who normally resented old-line regular army commanders.

Dwight D. Eisenhower, the man who would be von Rundstedt's opposite number, once the offensive began, was an individual of a far different stamp. Smiling and friendly, he was the typical product of the happy-go-lucky American civilization. Almost a genius at the hor-

173

rendous task of getting the opposing personalities of a Grand Alliance to work together, his greatest strength was organization rather than strategy.

Eisenhower, though trained in the regular professional military tradition, preferred to depend heavily on staff analysis. A *carry-outer* rather than a *thinker-upper*, he failed to react swiftly enough when the chips were down, some said, and this might have caused a disastrous lapse.

Luckily for the Allied cause, the echelon immediately below him—Bradley, Patton and Montgomery—reacted by instinct. And that instinct helped save the battle.

And to make it even worse, Ike had been through it all before. In Africa, during the early days of fighting, he had committed raw, unblooded troops against veterans. At Kasserine Pass, he had walked into an almost identical trap. There, the British 8th Army, advancing with hysterical speed from the south had saved his army. And the official scapegoat, Fredenall, had saved his name.

The tense, critical days of the Ardennes Battle—and the retrospective judgment of history—show that von Rundstedt was the best man for the job at hand. It was not von Rundstedt's planning or his leadership that caused the failure of the drive. The campaign failed for other reasons.

Nor can it be truthfully said that American command or staff work turned the tide.

Actually, Gerd von Rundstedt succeeded in thoroughly out-thinking and surprising the Allied Supreme Commander. In short, he constructed an intricate, elaborate mousetrap—and succeeded in drawing Ike Eisenhower into it!

How the German army managed to accomplish its incredible degree of total surprise and early victories is one of the great wonders of World War II.

In order to launch the offensive, it was necessary for von Rundstedt and *Feldmarschall* Walter Model, commander of German Army Group B to move—and to

174

concentrate—tremendous numbers of men and quantities of matériel in a relatively small area.

On the opening day of the offensive alone, von Rundstedt's plan called for hurling seventeen divisions—over 200,000 soldiers—against a narrow sector of the American line!

Behind this huge striking force—ready to move up and consolidate early gains—would stand more than a dozen reserve divisions. This tremendous mass of men was organized into three Field Armies—the Sixth Panzer under Dietrich, the Fifth Panzer under Manteuffel and the Seventh Army commanded by Brandenberger.

Needless to say, it was a tremendous task to amass the tanks, guns, ammunition and supplies necessary for this force. Military analysts find their credulity sorely tested by the grim fact that neither Allied Air Reconnaissance nor Allied Intelligence ever suspected that anything new or different was afoot!

To make matters ever more unbelievable, certain preliminary orders issued by the German high command in preparation for the offensive actually fell into the hands of Allied Intelligence! As early as October and November, 1944, G-2 sections at various levels were in possession of German communications which gave ample warning of the forthcoming build-up and attack. Yet absolutely nothing was done with this information—it was not even relayed to field units! And so it happened . . .

The Allied Armies had pulled up after a swift race across France. A halt was considered necessary to permit logistics and communications to catch up to the combat troops. Part of the Allied line ran through the Ardennes forest region of Belgium.

Unmindful—or rather unaware—of the German build-up taking place behind the enemy's lines, the Anglo-American command had few troops in the sector extending from Luxembourg in the south to St. Vith in the north.

Holding positions along the Schnee Eifel, a commanding hill-mass east of St. Vith, was the green, untried

106th Infantry Division. That unit plus the 4th and 28th Divisions and two Combat Commands of the 9th Armored Division, were the only outfits holding a line against which von Rundstedt would threw no less than *eleven* divisions in the first hours of the battle!

The German leaders had worked a miracle. Despite incessant Allied air raids against the Reich and its industry, they had collected nearly 5000 aircraft to use in the offensive. In addition to the new planes, among them ME-262 jets, the Nazi war machine in the west had been equipped with new tanks and artillery pieces in large numbers.

All this equipment had been brought to the front under the very eyes of Allied Air Reconnaissance. For weeks, German roads leading to the front had been clogged with guns and vehicles. Some of the convoys had been spotted, true enough, and bombed and strafed. Yet, the majority got through.

"One of our biggest troubles was the air of wild optimism that pervaded SHAEF headquarters," is the off-the-record admission of a retired American general. "We'd sliced across France and the top brass figured that Germany was licked. Anyone suggesting that the Nazis had enough strength left to launch a counter-offensive would have been hooted down in the officer's mess!"

There were some combat commanders who suspected something was up. Veteran front-line officers sensed there was something in the wind. Mainly on their own initiative, many of them ordered their fuel and supply drums moved far back behind the forward positions—one of the strokes that eventually contributed to the German defeat.

The attack that came on December 16th nonetheless caught the American Army flat-footed.

The assault went off like clock-work—exactly as Gerd von Rundstedt had planned it. Gen. Hasso von Manteuffel's Fifth Panzer Army slammed into the unblooded 106th Division. The 106th went to pieces.

Observers even then found it difficult to understand

why such a raw unit—the 106th had only recently arrived from the States—had been assigned a key holding position. The result of an attack against the division should have been a foregone conclusion.

In experience, men and officers were no match for Hitler's hardened veterans. The 106th broke—and large segments of it ran—and two regiments, the 422nd and 423rd, were all but completely wiped out.

To the south of the 106th, two entire German Corps struck the "Bloody Bucket" 28th Division—*which was holding more than twenty-seven miles of the front!*

Evidently, the heady perfume of victorious optimism still clogged the nostrils of the brass at SHAEF. Although seventeen Nazi divisions had been committed in the opening stages of the battle, the reports from the front were shrugged off by SHAEF intelligence sections.

"Just a local diversion," one top-level SHAEF G-2 officer decided.

Gerd von Rundstedt's reports were received with jubilation in Berlin.

"I told the Fuehrer on the first day of attack that surprise had been completely achieved," Col. Gen. Alfred Jodl stated after the war. "The best indication was that no reinforcements were made in your sector before the attack."

The German drive overwhelmed the thinly-spread American defense forces in the Ardennes. The line was pushed back. Regiments and divisions, outnumbered and outgunned, were forced to fall back. For more than forty-eight hours, SHAEF seemed in a state of paralysis.

Fearful rumors spread and what had been optimism turned to gloom—and then to a state almost bordering on hysteria. Even ranking officers were carried away by the wave of defeatism that swept the rear areas.

"The Germans are unbeatable . . ."

"We'll be licked . . ."

"They'll have us fighting with our backs to the sea . . ."

First the German strength and potential had been under-estimated. Now, it was over-estimated.

Despite the showing it was making in the Ardennes,

177

the slender resources of the *Wehrmacht* had been stretched beyond the breaking point. Fuel—for ground vehicles and aircraft—was the most serious shortage.

One of the most vital points in von Rundstedt's planning called for swift movement—*blitz* thrusts through the American line—for the purpose of capturing U.S. fuel and oil dumps. Without this, he knew the drive could not be sustained. The *Panzer* divisions had gasoline for only a few days—there were no reserves of gas left in Germany.

It is here that the foresight—almost bordering on occult perception—of the American field commanders paid off. Their action in moving their supply dumps to the rear denied the critically needed gasoline to the Nazis.

The Battle of the Bulge was fought at the divisional, regimental, battalion and company levels. In the confusion and chaos that followed the first day, the courage and determination of front-line units saved the situation, rather than any "Big-Picture" strategic or tactical moves or decisions emanating from SHAEF.

Fierce defensive actions were fought at St. Vith by Brig. Gen. Bruce Clarke and his Combat Command B of the 7th Armored Division and at Bastogne, where airborne troopers were completely surrounded and cut-off.

These stands, as well as others, slowed the German drive and ruined von Rundstedt's carefully planned time-table. The delaying actions were essential—for it was not until December 22nd that George Patton's Third Army brought the full weight of its counterpunch against the south side of the Bulge. It was also about that time that the weather cleared enough for Allied Air to resume large-scale operations.

Patton's attack and the resumption of air assaults sealed the fate of von Rundstedt's offensive, but it was not until mid-January that the Allies were able to start a drive to recapture lost ground.

There is an old saw among military men to the effect that one side's strategical success if automatically the other's strategical blunder. If this were accepted at face value, then the Battle of the Bulge would be a textbook example to illustrate the theory.

Using the opposing commanders—von Rundstedt and Eisenhower—as the representative single symbols of the two armies which faced each other in the Ardennes, one must arrive at an inescapable conclusion.

The German general clearly achieved all the elements of strategic superiority. Through his planning and command, entire corps and fantastic masses of weapons and equipment were brought to a front-line sector from widely-separated areas without serious hitch and, more importantly, without the knowledge of the Allies.

The assault was a complete surprise. Conceived as a last-ditch measure, the counteroffensive was brilliantly executed and stood an excellent chance of succeeding up to the very last.

General Dwight Eisenhower's intelligence service was faulty to the point of being virtually worthless in the period before and during the early stages of the battle. SHAEF G-2 was completely in the dark about German intentions—and grossly miscalculated enemy intentions and strength in the opening days of the Ardennes conflict.

In addition, it would almost appear that Eisenhower's staff was unnerved by the implications of the Bulge. Starting with such decisions as those placing the unreliable 106th Division in a vital position and which spread divisions like the 28th over great stretches of front, SHAEF staff-work does not stand up under close scrutiny.

Decisions to shift other units to the Bulge to throw back the Nazis seemed slow in coming. Several days elapsed before the full implication of the drive was realized and sufficient force diverted from other sectors to plug the gaps.

The coldly calculated offensive engineered by Gerd von Rundstedt, the stern-visuaged Prussian, ended in defeat. It nearly ended differently, however. For von Rundstedt had built a trap—an excellent trap—and he had enticed Dwight Eisenhower into it.

179

Luckily for the Allies, although Ike walked into the trap, he had enough power and punch to fight his way out eventually. Otherwise, the story of World War II might have had an entirely different ending. . . .

# THE DAY THEY BOMBED CASSINO

## By Russell F. Wallace

THE SCREAMING almost made me sick to my stomach. I hunched myself up tighter, dragging myself even lower behind the boulder. Carlson was lying out there, fifty, maybe sixty yards away—lying on his back with the blood pouring out of his belly by the quart.

"Shoot him! Goddamn it, why doesn't somebody put the poor slob out of his misery?" I heard Sergeant Anscomb curse—crouched and helpless, he was pressed in tightly against the sheer wall of the cliff.

*But they didn't shoot.* They let him lie there, screaming in agony, his life spurting out of him with every yell of pain. And they *laughed.* I could hear them, their gutteral voices shouting to us in broken English, asking us why we didn't go out to help our pal.

Fine chance. They had the small clearing so completely zeroed in that it was suicide to even approach Carlson. He was kicking weakly, his voice hoarse and thin. The screams became feeble, as his life ran out of him. He'd tried to help a pal, and they'd shot him—*cold-bloodedly* —in the belly.

I looked around. *Five of us*—all that was left of the whole platoon. We were five stinking dogfaces, tied up in knots, grounded, trapped, and afraid to move. The minute we did, we'd be clay pigeons in a shooting gallery.

Carlson's screaming stopped. For a second there was quiet—but only for a second. All around us, to the left and right, and way down below, the rifles were cracking steadily. Now and then, above the whine of the rifle fire was the raucous chatter of a heavy machine gun.

181

Anscomb waved and pointed down. *This was it.* Bug out—scram. Get down the mountain—*if we could.*

I gestured to the open space—a wide, clear plateau behind me. I couldn't cross it. I was scared stiff. I didn't want to end up like Carlson—a piece of riddled, bawling flesh, barely alive and with nothing to look forward to but a few minutes of horrifying pain and then . . . death.

"C'mon Wally, move! Over here. Run, dammit!" Anscomb waved frantically.

I sucked in my breath. My stomach hardened into a knot as I steeled myself. You've *got to,* I told myself. You've damned well got to. Now get on with it. *Move!*

I jumped up, hardly conscious of the movement. My mind and body were working in a haze. I didn't want to look. I didn't want to know. All I let myself be conscious of was that I had to move—*fast.* After a few seconds I heard the ground crackle. I felt the whoosh of air and heard the whine as a lead slug whistled past my cheek . . . *a fraction of an inch away.*

Anscomb shouted at me. "C'mon! Only a little more. Yout got it made, boy. Hurry!"

And then I felt his arm reaching out, grabbing me, pulling me in tightly to the cliffside. Under the tiny overhanging ledge, the two of us were hidden from the Germans—*for the moment.*

"Good boy! Sit down and catch your breath. You're going to need it." He pushed against me, literally forcing me to the ground. "We gotta get outa here, *and soon.* Captain Thatcher and the Third Platoon are down there. We gotta get back and join them before they bug out too. Or else we'll find ourselves walkin' all the way back to the MLR by ourselves."

It was supposed to be the big "cake walk," the easy climb to the top—the finish of that lousy, rotten battle.

Instead, it turned out to be a nightmare straight out of hell, an operation that was cursed from the word go. *We never had a chance.* Worse, we walked right into it like a pack of blind men off on a picnic. We'd made the biggest mistake that any bunch of infantrymen *could* make. We'd taken a job for granted. We'd let our own sweet-talking propaganda boys put us into a dreamworld. We'd listened to what they said on the radio, instead of trusting to our own, hard-earned combat experience. And we'd paid for the mistake—*but good.*

We'd been sitting in front of Monte Cassino for months. We'd rolled along at a fairly decent pace after we'd landed in Italy. Sure, there had been hard fighting, but nothing that we couldn't overcome. And then, slowly but surely, the advance had ground to a crawl. Every step meant blood and death. But we moved.

We'd moved until we'd run into Monte Cassino, that is. We could have taken that too, if it hadn't been for "political" reasons.

Even the best infantry needs help—meaning artillery. The enemies' big guns have to be silenced; concentrations of mortars and machine guns have to be knocked out; pockets of fanatical resistance must be destroyed. The dogfaces can't do it alone. They're only one part of a team.

*But we weren't permitted to shell Monte Cassino.*

The top of the mountain was crowned by an ancient Abbey, supposedly built by St. Bernard himself, the same Saint whom the great Swiss rescue dogs are named after. Aside from its value as a religious relic, the Abbey was important politically. For we had boasted that, unlike the Nazis, who had no feeling at all for hallowed places, *we* respected them, whether they belonged to friend or foe. We were "civilized."

The Germans caught on quickly. They covered the mountain with troops and set up elaborate defensive positions, concentrated around the Abbey. The Abbey buildings themselves were taken over by the German command and were transferred into an artillery observation post.

We were down in the valley. They were up above, literally looking down our throats. A man couldn't move a hundred feet in the open without having the Jerries spot him and start shooting.

We sat there helplessly, *taking it.* We could have gone up, as I said, with help. The Germans weren't well dug in. They couldn't be. Men can't do much digging in solid rock.

But every time we started to climb the hill, artillery and mortars zeroed down on us and cut us to pieces. At that time, we could have done the job with just a little help. *We didn't get it.* Later on, the Nazis made their defenses almost impregnable—nothing short of a full scale attack on a division or corps level could have had the slightest effect.

That was in the winter of 43-44. The Italian front was the major American push in Europe. The invasion of France—D-Day—was still months away. The entire prestige of Allied arms was at stake. *But we were going no place in a hurry.*

I remembered back to the morning, a million years before. Captain Thatcher briefed us on the mission. Why, he had even smiled when he told us about it. He was as excited as a schoolboy just before the Christmas holidays.

"They're going to bomb the Abbey, boys," he grinned. "It's all set. They just gave it to us at battalion. The B-17's are coming over in waves. Hundreds of them, they say. They're going to knock that damned German sanctuary right off the top of the mountain. There won't be enough Jerries left alive up there to stop a one-man patrol."

"When's the strike, Captain?" asked Lieutenant Brenner.

"It's forming up right now." The captain looked at his watch. "The first wave should be here in minutes. As soon as the last planes have dropped their loads, we shove off. It's a big one today, boys—the whole division is in on it. We're going up that mountain, and this time we're not going to come down again. *It's for real.*"

"Brenner," he continued, "your platoon will take the point. Lieutenant Caterani, your platoon will follow Brenner on the right flank. I'll be with the third platoon. We'll be in support. And Anscomb, keep me in sight. That's your job, got it? Don't get out of contact."

"What happens if we run into a fire fight?" asked Brenner. "Is Anscomb under me, or is he with you?"

"If there's a fire fight, and mind you I don't think there will be—not if the fly boys do the job battalion tells me they're going to do—but *if* there is one—all bets are off. Anscomb sticks with his platoon. But we'll be right there behind you, just in case. OK, any questions?"

Once we had the mission straight, we broke up to watch the show. And that's what it was—a big, beautiful show. I never saw anything so wonderful. The sky was filled with them. I'd never seen so many planes before in my life.

Just a mile away, the bleak, rocky monster of Monte Cassino was turning a bright fire red. My mouth fell open in awe. I could hardly believe what I saw. Little dots— so many that I couldn't even begin to count them—were trickling down out of the sky like lazy black feathers. They appeared to float there, drifting toward the earth so slowly that it seemed like hours before they finally landed.

Then, at the bottom, where they disappeared from view, big, red rosettes of flame leapt up toward the sky.

Seconds later, the noise of the explosions reached us. It was like thunder, peal after peal, each one adding to the one that came before. Soon the noise was so unbearable that I had to cover my ears.

It didn't stop. The planes kept coming—I didn't believe that there could be so many in the whole world. I wondered how the mountain itself could stand it. It seemed as if the blast of the millions of tons of high explosive would tear the rocks apart.

No one, no one at all thought that it was possible for anyone to survive the bombing. It was impossible for flesh and blood to take it—*and live.*

Then it was over. The final squadron winged over the Abbey, waggled its wings, banked and headed south again. The Air Force had won the battle. Now it was the "easy task" of the "occupation troops" to take over.

We started off as if we were going to a picnic. It was like a route march. The fellows sloughed along, taking it easy, joking and laughing. One wise GI even cracked, "Maybe they'll make us test our gas masks."

Ed Peabody was carrying a small portable radio, tuned in to AFR. We grinned as we heard them read the communique. The Air Force has "totally destroyed" the last

185

remnants of resistance on Monte Cassino and wiped out the Abbey.

We passed the first mile without incident—it was quiet and peaceful. Up on the hillside, a few birds began chirping. For that mountain at least, it seemed to us, the war was over. There'd be another hill, and another fight—but that was a job for another day. But that day, right then, there was nothing left to be afraid of. We straightened up a little, walking as if we were safely back home.

*We didn't even hear the shot.* Peabody just keeled over, soundlessly. The little radio dropped from his hand and clattered down into a tiny gulley beside the path. I dropped down beside him and rolled him over. The neat little hole through his forehead told the story. *Even for a sniper, it was damn good shooting.*

"Spread out! Get moving!" It was the lieutenant shouting orders at us.

"There he is. Up there!" Anscomb dropped flat, took a bead and fired. There was a flashing movement. "Got him."

We were at the base of the mountain and started up. We climbed ten meters, twenty, fifty, a hundred. *Still there was no sign of life.*

*Whoo - - - sh!* The whole upper face of Monte Cassino erupted in a roar of explosive violence. They had us cold—dead to rights—zeroed. Two machine guns chopped up the ground, traversing down, right into the center of the platoon.

*I didn't look. I didn't think.* I just bent my head and ran—straight ahead. Impossible to run up a mountain? It's easy—*when lead is chopping every living thing around you into mangled pieces of bloody flesh.*

I hardly saw where I was going until I ran smack into the side of a cliff. I sat down, *hard.* Anscomb, Carlson and Murphy came rushing up behind me.

Below us, we could see the remains of the platoon, struggling to get out of the line of fire, to take any kind of cover they could find. But those damned machine guns kept firing. They must have had every inch of low ground under observation.

"We gotta get that nest! It's over there somewhere. It can't be very far, either." The sergeant pointed over to the left, around the cliff face.

"OK, I'll go," I said.

"I'm with you, corp," volunteered Carlson.

"No, we're all in on it," announced the sergeant. "Look Murphy, you cover while we work around. I'll take the front, Carlson goes around to the right and Wally takes the left."

"Hell no, Anscomb," shot back Murphy. "They got the looie in that last burst. I saw him get it. That puts you in charge. You stay back and cover. Besides, you know you're a better shot than I am."

Without waiting for an answer, Murphy crawled away from the cliff face and started zigzagging forward again. Carlson and I moved out after him.

Then I saw them. They were almost completely hidden, lying in a crater that the bombs had dug out of the rock. *Murphy was almost on them.*

He had a grenade in his hand. The pin was pulled and his arm was swinging back to heave it. Then I heard Carlson shout at the top of his lungs, "Murphy, above you. Look out!"

I switched my glance for a second. Thirty or forty yards away, a German was raising up out of another crater, taking dead aim on Murphy. Even as I watched, he fired. Murphy stood there, like a statue, and then toppled over—I don't even know if he was still alive when the grenade went off, *underneath him.* I shuddered at the sound of the explosion. Pieces of flesh and dirty bits of uniform spattered high through the air.

The warning shout to Murphy alerted the Krauts to Carlson. The machine gun swiveled around, bearing directly on the youngster. There was no use shouting. The knuckles on the gunner's hands were already whitening. Carlson would be cut in half before the words could get out of my throat.

I had a grenade in my hand. I lobbed it, and saw it fall. The machine gun started to chatter—just a little— and then—*wham!* The ground shook under my body.

There was a burst of flame, a long scream—the chattering stopped.

A slug chopped the dirt beside my face. I rolled over. There was another spurt, another whine. The Jerries had me in their sights. I jumped up and ran toward a boulder behind me.

Then I heard it—those pitiful screams of pure animal pain. Carlson! He was lying out there with half a dozen machine gun slugs in his belly! *And I was trapped.*

I looked around. Anscomb was over by the cliff where we'd left him—down below were a few other figures—one, two, three of them. Three of them, and Anscomb and I made five—*all that were left out of the whole platoon.*

The whole mountain was literally swarming with Jerries! But this time, instead of lying out in the open, fighting against us on even terms, they were hidden, spotted away in man-made foxholes, foxholes so strong and so well built that only a direct grenade hit could wipe each one out. The foxholes were built for them in the bed rock of Monte Cassino—carved out, courtesy of the United States Air Force!

How we made it down that mountainside, I'll never know. But I've got to hand it to Anscomb. His nerves were like ice. If it hadn't been for him, I think I'd have gone to pieces before we'd moved a hundred yards.

We had to clear out another maching gun nest before we rejoined the captain's platoon. Anscomb handled that one, *as neat as you please.* The Germans never knew what hit them. They were concentrating so hard on the captain's group, that they never even suspected that there was anyone behind them. I suppose they figured that our bunch was all gone—to the last man. It just goes to show that overconfidence can work both ways.

Anscomb was within spitting distance before they even knew anything was happening. And when one German did turn around, I let him have it before he even got over staring. No one else had a chance to spot anything, because along about that time Anscomb let loose with a pair of grenades. End of machine guns.

We crawled back to our jump-off area, *what was left*

*of us.* From what I saw and heard, the rest of the division took pretty much the same sort of treatment that we did. We never did take Monte Cassino that day—or the next day—or the next month.

With the fortifications that the bombardment had dug for them, the Germans set up a pretty rugged defensive system. I'd hate to estimate how many lives were lost before that one stinking monster of a mountain was finally taken.

That's war. It stinks no matter how you look at it. But bad as it is, it gets even worse when fellows who don't understand the problem take a hand.

I've got nothing against the Air Force. In their own way, they did—and still do a swell job. But when it comes to ground fighting, they're strictly in the way. Because when you get to a mountain, brother, there's only one way to reach the top. *Start walking, pal—start walking.*

# Three Big 35¢ Books for $1.00—Postage Free

**214** (35¢) **COME-ON GIRL,** Stuart Friedman. A girl who would do anything for kicks—in a gambling town where everything goes.

**221** (35¢) **VICE-COP,** Richard Deming. "They started with thrill parties and ended with murder." By the author of the famous *Dragnet* novels.

**L503** (50¢) **SEX LIFE OF THE MODERN ADULT,** Dr. Leland E. Glover. Now available at last! The Glover Report, based on a psychologist's actual files.

**L506** (50¢) **THE SECRET AGENT'S BADGE OF COURAGE,** Ernest Hemingway. The World's Greatest Spy Stories, with gems by Eric Ambler, Pearl Buck, Joseph Conrad.

**L507** (50¢) **MEET THE MOB,** Detective Mullady and Bill Kofoed. "A great book!" —Oscar Fraley, co-author, *The Untouchables.* 16 pages of photos.

**L509** (50¢) **THE BATTLE OF LEYTE GULF,** Stan Smith. "The greatest battle in the history of naval warfare."—*Time.* Official U. S. Navy photos.

**227** (35¢) **THE BORGIA BLADE,** Gardner F. Fox. The best-selling historical novel about romance and revenge in the most corrupt court of Europe.

**229** (35¢) **TEN AGAINST THE THIRD REICH,** Stan Smith. True accounts of the smashing of Nazi Germany from within.

**L510** (50¢) **MOST LIKELY TO SUCCEED,** John Dos Passos. Controversial novel by the author of best-selling *Midcentury.*

**L511** (50¢) **THE TRAITOR,** W. Somerset Maugham. Classics of espionage, with the amazing *"Eichmann: The Hunter and the Hunted."*

**L512** (50¢) **THE SHADOW IN THE ROSE GARDEN,** D. H. Lawrence. Great tales of passion, ed. from *Bachelor's Quarters.*

**L513** (50¢) **HOW TO GET RICH BUYING STOCKS,** Ira U. Cobleigh. The amazing Wall Street Guide to 500% *profits!*

**230** (35¢) **CREEPS BY NIGHT,** Dashiell Hammett. 10 weird masterpieces, classics of horror literature.

**231** (35¢) **MY LIFE AND LOVES IN GREENWICH VILLAGE,** Maxwell Bodenheim. The famous uninhibited "Coffeehouse Diary."

**L514** (50¢) **SINATRA AND HIS RAT PACK,** Richard Gehman. The irreverent, unbiased, uninhibited book about Frank and "The Clan."

**L515** (50¢) **MEMOIRS,** Admiral Karl Doenitz. The Nazi documentary no other man could write—"An important war document"—*Sat. Review.*

**232** (35¢) **THE DAY THE WAR ENDS,** Irwin Shaw. Exciting battlefield stories from the $3.95 best-seller *Civilians Under Arms,* ed. Herbert Mitgang.

**233** (35¢) **NIGHTMARES,** Robert Bloch. By the author of *Psycho*—"Horror as ruddy-cheeked as a fresh gorged vampire"—*N. Y. Herald Tribune.*

**234** (35¢) **LOVE DOCTOR,** Florence Stonebraker. The best-selling novel of a man who violated the code of his profession.

**235** (35¢) **A GUN FOR CANTRELL,** Harry Sinclair Drago. The master western novelist's roaring story of the great range war.

**236** (35¢) **MARKHAM,** Lawrence Block. The case of the pornographic photos: novel from TV's great suspense series, starring Ray Milland.

**237** (35¢) **STRONGER THAN FEAR,** Richard Tregaskis. Extraordinary World War II novel by the author of world-famous *Guadalcanal Diary.* "Grim and true and very realistic"—*N. Y. Times.*

**L516** (50¢) **THE AMBASSADOR,** Aldous Huxley. Sophisticated stories of passion: "The erotic in classic literature."

**L517** (50¢) **EAT YOUR TROUBLES AWAY,** Dr. Lelord Kordel. Health and virility for men and women of all ages. Includes the famous 15-Day Rejuvenation Diet.

**L518** (50¢) **COME INTO MY PARLOR,** Charles Washburn. The uninhibited classic about the house of the Everleigh Sisters. "Sin deluxe in the *Roaring 20's.*"

**L519** (50¢) **KHRUSHCHEV'S "MEIN KAMPF,"** background by Harrison E. Salisbury, specialist in Soviet Affairs, *N. Y. Times.* The dictator's own official blueprint for world conquest.

**238** (35¢) **13 AGAINST THE RISING SUN,** Stanley E. Smith. The inside true stories of the blood-and-guts battles fought by the Marines and GI's in the war against Japan.

**239** (35¢) **THE RED BRAIN,** Dashiell Hammett. "10 creepy stories, with mixed ingredients of shock and horror"—Dr. Leland E. Glover.

www.ingramcontent.com/pod-product-compliance
Lightning Source LLC
LaVergne TN
LVHW091254080426
835510LV00007B/261